Whatever Happened to

Molly Murphy's

House of

Fine Repute?

Jeffiee Tayar

First published by Dog Ear Publishing
4010 W. 86th Street, Ste H
Indianapolis, IN 46268
www.dogearpublishing.net

ISBN: 978-159858-519-3

This book is printed on acid-free paper.

Printed in the United States of America

Dedication

TO ALL OF MOLLY'S KIDS,
who were the heart of
Molly Murphy's House of Fine Repute,
especially "Klinger" and "French Maid"

Contents

This book is supported by Public and Court Records.

Part I

The Beginning

People still remember the good times they had at Molly Murphy's House of Fine Repute even though it has been closed since January 1, 1996. When new acquaintances learn that my deceased/former husband and I owned Molly's, their first response is, "Oh, we used to LOVE that place!" The second response is, "Whatever happened to it?" That can't be answered in 30 words or less, so here is what happened to Molly Murphy's House of Fine Repute, as I remember it.

Since it was the product of Bob Tayar, I'll begin my story with the first time I laid eyes on the man. That was in the fall of 1960. I was 19 years old and had moved to "The City" from Ardmore, Oklahoma, where I graduated from high school in 1959. Ardmore was a very wealthy oil town, but we weren't part of that census. Daddy was employed by the Civil Service, and we were in Ardmore because it was home to the Gene Autry Air Force Base. (I'll never forget the embarrassment I felt when the teacher would make us kids of Civil Servants raise our hands to identify ourselves, so the school could get their government money.)

In my family, we three daughters were not expected to go to college after graduation. We were expected to go to "The City," get a job in an office, and find a husband. As long as he was white and had a job, any man would qualify. I was last in line and following in my two older sisters' footsteps. My office job was as an entry level filing clerk at Wesley Hospital - pay $160 a month. Some people will read that and say, "Well, that was a lot of money back then." NO! It was NOT a lot of money back then. It was not enough to even pay the $7 a week rent at the YWCA, buy bus fare, meals, and an office wardrobe. The first thing to be omitted before payday was meals. If I didn't have a date, I didn't eat. Bus fare came next. Many times I walked the mile down Hudson from Wesley Hospital to the YWCA in pointed toe, high heeled shoes. (No wonder I have such bad feet now!) My weekly trip to the beauty salon was far more important than food or bus fare. My bee-hive hairdo got put in place on Fridays and never a hair on my head moved until the next Friday, when it was washed, re-teased, and sprayed with lacquer to make it hold for another 7 days. Those bee-hives were wrapped with toilet paper before going to bed at night to keep them perfect all week.

Though I was still a teenager, I was employed full time in an office, so naturally I socialized with older women who were also employed there. One of my co-workers introduced me to her friend, Roger Sarfaty. Roger was about 10 years older, had a full head of beautiful white hair, smoked skinny cigars, and was a professional gambler, mostly on bridge. I went out with him a few times and felt so very worldly and mature. I even took up smoking Marlboros in a futile attempt to look sophisticated. Actually, I looked like a 19 year old, chubby cheeked, innocent girl smoking a cigarette.

One Sunday evening Roger took me to The Shangra La Club on 23rd Street, near the Capitol. It was a very popular nightclub. In those days selling liquor was against the law so you had to be known by the bartender or carry your brown bag containing spirits and pour your drinks under the table. Some bars would sell a private club membership card for $1 and claim to be a private club and sold cocktails only to people owning one of those exclusive membership cards. I don't recall exactly how The Shangra La operated, but it was about the nicest nightclub in town at that time. Also, as long as I was with an older man, I was never ID'd.

Roger and I were sitting, enjoying a Whisky Sour, when a tall, very thin, dark haired man walked over to our table. Seems Roger had gone to school with this man, and he was introduced to me as Bob Tayar. Bob was well groomed and had a Lebanese nose, but still attractive. (I learned later that he weighed 130 pounds at that time…and so did I!) When Roger excused himself to go to the men's room, Bob asked me to dance. The song was slow, and he was doing some step I didn't know how to do, like maybe a Fox Trot. I had only learned the Box Step and the Jitterbug in Ardmore High. However, someone had told me, that if you dance close, you can follow any dance step. So, I thought that was what I was doing. Bob interpreted my close dancing as a "come-on." He decided I must be "easy" so he made a mental note to phone me at the Y for a date. I know this to be true because he told the story later on radio station KGB in San Diego to my niece, Shelly Dunn, on her morning show, except he used more graphic words to describe how I was dancing. Thank God I knew very few people in San Diego to hear that story.

Having been advised by the Big Girls never to date two men who were friends, I declined his offers and set him up with my girlfriends and we double dated. After a few months of that, we finally just began dating each other.

I recall one evening we were driving on Classen Boulevard, on our way to Fuzzy's Club when he said he needed to tell me about his birth. He was Syrian. Now, I was from a small town and had never heard of Syrians, Jews, or any other minority except Indians and Negroes, so I thought he was telling me his mother had a Caesarean Section when she gave birth to him. I assured him that was fine with me and wondered why on earth he would think I'd be interested!

He also told me he was 26 years old. I told him I was 21. OK. We were both lying. He was 29, and I was 19, but by the time the truth was known, it didn't matter.

Bob had just gone broke in a little hamburger spot in downtown Oklahoma City and didn't have a penny. He lived with his mother who was in her mid-70's, drove a blue Nash Rambler with a dented front fender and worked on commission in a men's clothing store. Though neither of us had any money, we dressed and acted as though we did. About this time Jack Sussy opened a fabulous place, The Nomad Club on Lincoln. Jack was the New Yorker who moved to Oklahoma and introduced pizza to Oklahomans. The Nomad was THE place to be seen and Bob loved the nightlife. Bob knew every bartender, every musician, and every cocktail waitress at all the popular places in Oklahoma City. He was just a "night" person. In fact, he was so NOT a morning person his mother had shipped him off to Oklahoma Military Academy for high school because she couldn't get him out of bed in the mornings to go to high school classes. At that time military school was considered detention for rich kids. Bob wasn't a rich kid, but he was exposed to their lifestyle there. His friends were the rich kids, and he was the hot tempered Arab who ran with them.

Being so educated on the local nightlife scene, Bob concluded that this city needed a Dixieland place, like The Levee, he saw in Dallas. He found a location on 10th Street, across from the fairgrounds, where there used to be a baseball field, and borrowed $3,000 from his brother who owned a grocery store. This $3,000 paid for red leather, tufted booths, a bar and a sign with the words, "Sewanee Club" written on it. This was in 1962. The place looked good enough, and the Dixieland Band was terrific but there weren't enough beer drinkin', Dixieland lovin' customers to pay the overhead.   Bob, being impatient and needing a better cash flow, changed the band to a black trio who were well known around town. The group was comprised of a drummer, Freddie, piano player, Roosevelt, and a singer, Clay. Clay did a rendition of "Bill Bailey, Won't You Please Come Home" that brought the house down. She would actually be lying on the floor, kicking her feet up in the air, wailing into her microphone for that man to return! A dance floor was added that was round, made of white tiles, with black seams, making it appear to be a giant baseball. The Sewanee sign was changed to "The Dugout Club." Business was better but only on the weekends. To make any money we needed to be more than a weekend spot.

The fact that we weren't making any money didn't keep us from going on with our marriage plans. In March 1963, we married and had our reception at The Dugout Club. By this time I was working at Braniff Airlines as a reservationist, and we were able to use my free passes to go to Mexico City for our honeymoon. We were renting an apartment for $65 a month and just as happy as we could be, considering our income. Bob was so determined that he would support his wife that he wouldn't allow me to cash my paychecks from Braniff. They all went into a savings account so we could eventually make a down payment on a house. He was determined to earn a good living from this little club of his so he spent hours thinking of how to entice more customers. That was when he came up with the idea of strippers.

Bob and Jeffiee ca 1962 at The Dugout Club

I had never even seen a strip show until we were running them. It had been several years since there was a strip club in Oklahoma City so Bob found an agent, Ruth Sallee, who had girls on the Dallas, Kansas City, St. Louis circuit. He only wanted to try this new scheme on Thursday nights, to see how it went. The girls came to The Dugout just after leaving Jack Ruby's place in Dallas. (Yes, Jack Ruby, the man who shot JFK's assassin). Well, turned out, that is exactly what was needed to fill The Dugout Club. Since I worked the evening shift at Braniff and was off on Thursday and Friday nights, I could help at the club. I "worked" the door, which meant I checked IDs and collected $2 a person before anyone could enter the premises. I also kept a lookout for the Vice Squad.

Sometimes they got by me, and we would have to pay a fine for selling liquor by the drink, which was still illegal, but that was just considered a business expense. Since those Thursday Strip Nights were so successful, Bob added Friday and then Saturday nights. Needless to say, we would be packed all those nights. Then he came up with the idea of Amateur Night on Wednesday nights. "Earn While You Learn" was how our ad read in the help wanted section of the newspaper. I would talk with the girls, sometimes go pick them up, sell them pasties I made for $2 a set, and explain why I didn't strip myself. Again, those nights were wildly successful so Bob got another idea- female impersonators. No straight bar had them in Oklahoma.

Toni Sinclair was the best. He and his troupe were local hair-dressers who made gorgeous women. They had costumes that would knock your eyes out. Occasionally a male customer would be trying to buy one of them a drink and then be amazed, and embarrassed, when he found out they were actually men. Toni became my best girlfriend. I recall one morning, after closing at 2 a.m. we all went to Cattlemen's for breakfast. By this time Braniff had moved their reservation center to Dallas, and I was only employed by my husband. As we sat at the table, surrounded by female impersonators, musicians who were probably on drugs, and strippers who were probably prostitutes, I whispered to my husband, "God, look at the people we are socializing with." Toni overheard this comment and said, "You know, around this group I feel almost normal!"

These packed house weeks went on for several months. The $2 door charge had accumulated to about $40,000. Since it was all cash, we saw no reason to report it to the IRS. So we hid it in the freezer at home. That was until a Judge Korn was sent to prison for income tax evasion. Bob concluded that if a judge was sent to prison for a few years, he would be sent up for life! So, one afternoon we took a brown paper grocery sack and filled it with the $40,000 and took it to Jim Elder at May Avenue Bank to make a deposit. It was all in ones, fives, tens, and twenties. It took awhile for Jim to count it. This was the money that got us into the restaurant business.

We had used my Braniff salary savings and purchased a new house in the Edgewater addition on North Portland. This was an upper middle class neighborhood where all the homes had shake shingled roofs, stockade fences and a chimney showing above the rooftop. It was also in a very good school district and that was a consideration for us, since I soon became pregnant. We moved into this lovely neighborhood using a borrowed pick-up truck to transport our small amount of furniture ... you know, the Early Marriage style. We were out of the nightclub business due to a fire caused by a cigarette dropped in the wastebasket under the bar. Since Bob's goal was to open a restaurant, we didn't attempt to rebuild The Dugout.

Now most businessmen would have a coronary at the thought of erecting a $40,000 building on leased land, but Bob did just that. Harry Reeder owned a piece of land on N.W. 39th Expressway, the old U.S. 66 Highway. When we leased that land, I-40 had not opened yet so there was very good traffic. Unfortunately for us the interstate opened just after we did. There went all the out of state traffic that might stop in for a hamburger in our Charcoal Kitchen sailing right down I-40 on to Arkansas. So, we struggled. For six months we couldn't afford to pay our vendors, and I was pregnant, wearing white, maternity uniforms to work each day. We had a new house, sparsely furnished, a business losing money, and a baby on the way. No wonder I used to go home after working my 9-7 shift at the drive-in and cry from worry. Bob took the late shift. He arrived just in time for the lunch business, in case we actually had some, and closed up at midnight.

Shortly after we opened this drive-in restaurant we were hit with a lawsuit from the owner of The Charcoal Oven Drive In. Our building and grounds looked almost identical to his Charcoal Oven. The only difference was that we didn't have the cars lined up to place orders at our drive up speakers. We did win that lawsuit because, just as designer dresses can be copied, so can a building be copied.

Bob never claimed to have original ideas. Our menu was almost a replica of The Split-T, an Oklahoma City institution. Our food was just as good. That would be due to my going over and getting hired by Johnnie, the manager. I worked there for a couple of weeks and left with their cook, broiler man, and lead lineman. The cook had all the recipes, including their Hick'ry sauce and their onion ring batter. They were, and still are at Johnnie's Charcoaler, great!

During those long evening hours, waiting for a car to pull in our drive-way Bob would rack his brain trying to figure out how to get more business. He would watch car after car pass our drive and pull into Shakey's Pizza's lot next door. They were packed every night.

It was remarkable that Bob was able to put in another restaurant with all the debt we had, but he did. During those late '60s, Shepherd Mall had opened as the only enclosed mall in Oklahoma. There was an El Chico's Mexican Restaurant and Val Gene's Cafeteria there but no place selling hamburgers and fries. We had no money but the owner of the mall financed Bob's part and for the only time in his life, Bob took in a business partner. That partnership didn't last long before Bob bought him out, and we became the sole owners.

By the time we opened Bonapartes Charcoaler at Shepherd Mall and Bonaparte's Retreat, a small cocktail lounge in the back, our son had been born. My routine was to drop our baby at the nursery and work the lunch hour at the drive-in. On Bonaparte's opening day I had planned to go over to the mall and enjoy sitting down for lunch in our new restaurant. Was I ever surprised when I walked in to "kitchen chaos." I immediately went to the order station and began taking orders.

Bonaparte's had white, French style phones on each table and booth for the customers to phone in their orders, then be called back when the orders were ready for pick up. I did the interior decorating, and I am the first to admit I am NOT an interior decorator. I can copy however, so on one of our Las Vegas junkets I sat in the cocktail lounge of the Frontier Hotel and sketched the room. We just duplicated it in the mall. Business was booming. We finally had a profitable restaurant.

Bob then made another smart decision. He took our entire savings of $10,000 and had a huge neon, Las Vegas type sign built and erected in front of the drive-in proclaiming it now to be "Bonaparte's Drive-In." Crazy as it sounds, the minute the switch was turned on and that sign was lighted, cars began pulling in the drive and were lined up until closing. So, now we had two profitable businesses. For me, that meant I could finally furnish my house and be assured of being able to feed my baby.

Bob Tayar was bored with operations. He liked the excitement and anticipation of planning and building a restaurant. Once it opened, he would hire a manager to run it. He was a tough boss, but he was even worse with the customers. If a customer complained, he would tell them to just go on down to Val Gene's and eat. Bob realized he had this fault so he always tried to have a good general manager on site.

I was reminded recently of Bob's lack of public relations skills by Robert Goldman, an attorney, who represented a woman who sued us in the '70s. Seems she worked at the TG&Y next door to Bonaparte's at Shepherd Mall and she, like many mall employees, took one of our trays back to her store. Bob was tired of losing trays and coffee cups, so he had her arrested for theft. Well, he couldn't prove she took the tray so she sued him for false arrest. When the attorney asked Bob his income in order to set punitive damages, Bob refused to say. When pressed, he finally said, "Well, the sky's the limit." Robert Goldman thought how crazy Bob was to shoot himself in the foot and paying a large amount for punitive damages by not answering the question in a reasonable manner. He didn't understand Bob. We had insurance to pay the lawsuit, and Bob was not going to tell anything he didn't want to tell. Like Frank Sinatra, he simply did things HIS WAY.

With two successes it was much easier to expand. Casady Square was the next location for a Bonaparte's Charcoaler. We never made a penny in that location! In fact, the concept was changed five times, once with the infamous Jack Sussy serving his Italian specialties, and we still couldn't seat enough customers to create a positive cash flow. Eventually we got out from under that lease. But then there was Texas.

We put a Bonaparte's Charcoaler in Town East Mall in Mesquite, Texas, that did a fair volume of business, but the mall owners had also wanted a steakhouse there. So, we added one to appease them and called it "The Emperor's Table Steak House."

Our luck Texas had just passed Liquor by the Drink, but it was on county option, and this county where Town East Mall was located did not vote for it. But Dallas did, and all those potential steak eating customers would just drive another 20 minutes to the Dallas area where they could drink and dine. Six months and $250,000 later we were able to break that lease after proving the mall's security staff had been breaking in after hours and stealing steaks from our freezer.

We relinquished the apartment we had rented in Dallas for Bob to use during the time he spent there. I didn't use it much because I stayed in Oklahoma City and took care of those two stores, as well as our son who was in grade school now. On Sundays I would pick up the neighborhood children who were Lebanese and take them to St. Elijah's Orthodox Church for Sunday school. Bob's father, Elias Tayar, had helped build the church on 16th and Pennsylvania years earlier but Bob had never been a member. He felt it was time our son learn about his heritage and wanted him to grow up in the church. Being "Americana," or "white" as he referred to me, I was never quite comfortable there but still, I wanted us to have our place in the community, just as Bob did (and forget about those strip club beginnings).

The time Bob spent in the Dallas area was not wasted. Those nights after closing our restaurant he wasn't anxious to go to his empty apartment, so lovin' the night life, he made the rounds of the busiest places to study them and learn why they were so successful. The place he watched closely was Bobby McGee's Conglomerate. Bobby McGee's was a restaurant that had capacity crowds every night. They opened at 5 p.m. with a line waiting to be seated. The music was "up" and the disco dance floor was crowded. Hmmm...that means unlike our other restaurants that had to hire two shifts of employees, this Bobby McGee's only had one shift. And they didn't employ musicians, only one D.J. (Much less overhead there.) Everyone seemed to be having a great time and the food was very good. The menu was limited to about eight to ten items that would be cooked to order. No food waste. The décor was unusual. The salad bar was in a claw foot bathtub and the waiters were all dressed in crazy garbs. This was a unique restaurant! Naturally, Bob thought he should open a restaurant like this in

Oklahoma City and was wondering if I would be able to sketch this interior, when he heard of another place that was even better in San Antonio.

So off we went to The Magic Time Machine, which indeed, was better. The décor was wild and the waiters didn't just dress silly, they dressed as known characters, and assumed that persona all evening. On a scale of 1 to 10, Bobby McGee's was a 7 and The Magic Time Machine was a 10. Again, how on earth could I sketch all this and duplicate it in Oklahoma City? Thank God, we were able to locate the designer in Phoenix who said he could design an even better restaurant for us! He also told us to count on about $1 million as the investment.

Ok. We had two hamburger spots earning a decent living but there was that $250,000 debt hanging over our heads from that Texas disaster so any rational person would realize this new restaurant could never become a reality. Being rational was never a description of Bob Tayar.

After returning to Oklahoma City he found two locations; one on the north side of town and the other on South Meridian, just off I-40. I remember our taking a drive one evening, as we often did to check our drive-in business as well as that of our competitors, with our son asleep in the back seat, trying to decide which location would be the better. My opinion was the one on South Meridian because it was on the way to the airport and just as the area around Love Field in Dallas was surrounded with restaurants and motels, I thought this could be. At this time, it was just a vacant field with Shepler's Western Wear located next door. Bob always gave me credit for selecting this perfect site, but actually, if he had not liked it, it wouldn't have been built there.

Jim Scott owned that property and after taking him to San Antonio to see what we wanted to do, he agreed to "build to suit." OK. That got us a building but now we needed about $200,000 worth of equipment. Wayne Curtis had owned Curtis Equipment Company for several years and was an astute businessman. Bob and I visited him and he liked the fact that we worked together in our restaurants and agreed to co-sign our bank note for all the equipment. It was unbelievable! The next hurdle would be opening cash. There would be training of staff, stocking the bar, utilities before actually opening ... all those things take cash and our two little hamburger places couldn't afford to carry that burden.

All those saved Braniff paychecks that went into our house had given us a nice equity and we had been paying on the house for 10 years. Also, I had been making double payments ever since we had our first business success. In other words, the mortgage was almost paid off. As any entrepreneur would do, we refinanced our house to get the $30,000 for opening cash.

Nearly every evening that summer of 1975 we would drive our previously owned Cadillac El Dorado down 39th Expressway to check on Bonaparte's Drive In, then on down South Meridian to see the accomplishments the builder had made that day, with our son, Bobby, in the back seat. As we passed Sonic Drive In we would comment on how badly we felt for that poor woman who owned it and how business went down after her husband died. Of course, this was before some young man, I believe it was Stephen Lynn, bought it and turned it into a huge national chain of drive-ins.

That fall of 1975, I was so sure we were going to be successful I went to Shepler's and bought two suede pant suits that cost about $250 each. I wanted to be sure to have some good-lookin' clothes when we actually opened this new venture that we were sure would change our financial status. That restaurant would open on March 18, 1976, on Bob's 44th birthday. He wanted a name that sounded like a good time; one that was catchy; one people would remember. He named it "Molly Murphy's House of Fine Repute."

Photo of Jeffiee, Bob and Bobby at Molly's opening
Mar 17, 1976 in Oklahoma City.

Described by Playboy as "a Russian Orthodox Church
that mated with a ranch house".

The Molly Murphy's menu - late 70's until about 1982 or 1983, I would guess.

FORUM FOLLIES

An Oklahoma City woman, who has noted the curious cases we occasionally report in "The Playboy Forum" and who for professional reasons wishes to remain anonymous, passes along one that surely must have been a challenge for the plaintiff's attorney, Dan Zorn, to translate into a straight-faced legal complaint. Editing out only the names and dates, the petition alleges:

That the plaintiff and her date were guests at the defendant's restaurant for the purpose of having dinner at approximately eight P.M.

Plaintiff alleges that while she and her date were obtaining salads from the salad bar, a waiter who was working as an employee for the defendant came behind the plaintiff with a long horn, probably two to three feet in length, and while the plaintiff was obtaining a salad with her back turned to the defendant's employee, he took the open end of the horn and placed it between plaintiff's legs. Plaintiff alleges that the defendant's employee forced the horn up between plaintiff's legs, with the end of the horn touching plaintiff's vagina, and while in that position, proceeded to blow the horn. Plaintiff alleges that she was startled and greatly humiliated by the conduct of defendant's employee.

Plaintiff alleges that defendant's employee committed an assault and battery upon her person and that as a result of assault and battery, the plaintiff suffered great personal humiliation and embarrassment and shock and anxiety . . . and that plaintiff is entitled to punitive damages in the sum of $10,000. . . .

On advice of counsel—ours and the woman's—we will add that the matter was settled out of court for a reasonable sum that satisfied the plaintiff and presumably preserved the reputation of the defendant establishment, Molly Murphy's House of Fine Repute.

The waiter was "Harpo" - the horn was about 12 inches long. He simply honked his horn behind her as she was bending over the salad car.

Part II

Success!

Those months prior to opening Molly Murphy's I felt I knew a secret no one else knew. We were going to be rich! I was so sure of our future success that when Bob suggested we go ahead and plan a summer vacation at Newport Beach, California, I was all for it. The excitement and anticipation of Molly's were a natural high. We had pre-opening trial runs, inviting family and friends. I invited my English Professor, Dr. James Boren, and he brought his brother, Lyle Boren, our governor's father. We planned a press party for March 17th and invited VIPs, family, and friends. I will say, we had way more family than friends.

That night was absolutely perfect, except for when I spent time paying homage to that White Porcelain Goddess at Denny's Restaurant. The perfect planning was due not to Bob but to the general manager he had hired a couple of months earlier to run Molly's, Hank Kraft. Hank had just graduated from The University of Oklahoma and had some restaurant experience behind him. He stayed up all night long before opening and had the staff trained and had tested them before they could be on the floor. Their costumes had to be approved and they had to play their character to a "T". Not too many restaurants open that smoothly, but Hank was the best. That has been proven by the fact that after he left Molly's he teamed up with his friend, Hal Smith, and they now own somewhere in the neighborhood of 50 restaurants! All very successful.

As the guests entered the building, they were astounded at the décor. A toilet filled with flowers was placed next to the podium, a crystal chandelier hung in the entry, a mirror framed by antique door knobs decorated the front wall. Everywhere you looked there was some crazy décor. The bar had been covered with small pieces of broken mirror, then coated with resin. A boat hung over a booth, being driven by a stuffed monkey. One ceiling area had flower pots hanging upside down and booths were separated by bowling balls. It is impossible to describe the place in its entirety. Let's just say, it was the talk of the town.

Back to that White Porcelain Goddess ... I wanted to look really special and thin that night that I was deemed to become rich, so I didn't eat all day long. I had my hairdresser come by the house and do my make-up and hair, while the out of state Tayar relatives had cocktails in the living room. We all went to the press party where the salad car - that's right, salad **car**, a red XKE Jaguar convertible - was filled with shrimp. There were other things to nibble on, but I spent the evening walking around in a daze, sipping red wine. My friend, Rhonda, and I had our picture taken together and decided we looked like movie stars. Later in the evening the music was so good that I was on the dance floor thinking I was a really hot disco dancer making the cool moves to the popular songs, "I Believe In Miracles," ("Since you came along, you sexy thing") and "Oh, What A Night." Every time I hear those songs on the radio, I am taken back to that special night at Molly's. So, after being so high on excitement then on red wine, and not eating, when the 14 members of the extended Tayar family went over to Denny's for breakfast, I spent the time in the lady's room...on my knees. It wouldn't have been so bad if it had been over then but no...when we got home, before getting into the house, I got sick in the hedge by the porch. Our 10 year old son had never seen his Mom like that and asked what was wrong...his Dad told him his Mother was drunk! Thanks Bob.

The next morning I felt better, but when I looked at the 5 pounds of chicken livers that I was planning to fry, I wasn't sure I would make it. I did. I had the 14 members of the Tayar family over for a lovely brunch and we all agreed that Molly Murphy's House of Fine Repute was going to be a major success.

Indeed, it was a major success! On opening day, customers began lining up just after 4 o'clock, waiting to be the first diners in the new restaurant. Acquaintances I would run into at the grocery store would tell me they would wait until the lines shortened before they came down to dinner, but the lines didn't shorten for several years. Every night was a Saturday night. We seated 150 people in the dining room, 150 in the disco and about 20 in the waiting room. We normally served 800 to 900 people from 5 p.m. until closing. Closing was after everyone had been served. The flow was to wait outside for 30 minutes or so and our staff poured complimentary champagne, then maybe a 30 minute wait in the waiting room inside, and most likely an hour or more in the disco before getting into the dining room. But, once a party was seated in the dining room, they had excellent service, loads of fun, and great food. And besides, the wait was half the fun!

One staff member was designated as "entertainer." That person's responsibility was to get the party started. We had "Michael Jackson," "Elvis," and several others throughout the 20 years of operation whose job was getting the customer involved in the dance routines. And our DJs were all excellent at selecting danceable music and getting people on their feet. The staff had a few shows they would do, but mostly we wanted audience participation. "My Girl" was a crowd favorite. Three men would be selected from the crowd, given a sequined sport coat and sunglasses and told to follow the entertainer. Then they would do a hilarious impersonation of the Temptations and their famous song. The audience would be flashing their cameras and cheering as though they were watching rock stars.

The fun began immediately at our 5 p.m. opening. In order to get every member of the staff in a happy mood, the DJ would begin playing rock music about 4 p.m. The music was piped into the kitchen so all the staff was rockin'. (I have heard tales of some Maryjane being used also, but it was not condoned by the management.) Music was also on the speakers out front, where the cocktail waitresses and hosts would congregate next to the going home traffic on Meridian and do a dance routine, in their costumes. Aretha Franklin's "Freedom" was a traffic stopper. The drivers couldn't believe what they were seeing. Then at exactly 5 p.m. the DJ would play "The William Tell Overture," and we were open for business.

Diners were warned not to ask where the restrooms were. If some unsuspecting person should ask, immediately a Potty Call would be announced and a line formed, holding hands, weaving through the restaurant embarrassing the poor soul who had missed that warning. Occasionally the line would be taken over to the Wendy's restaurant, next door, to use their restroom. I don't believe even the best journalist could adequately describe the goings on at Molly's though Marian Hahn wrote a story that was featured in "**Milwaukee Area** Guide", in 1980. It read:

"….I entered alone while Warren was parking the car in the well-filled parking area surrounding the strange-looking building of tilted timber and stained glass portholes topped with a mosque-like dome.

"Shades of Friar Tuck!" said a hooded friar who greeted me, "What have we here?" He circled around me like a mosquito about to land. He picked up my handbag and pronounced it "Heavy, man, H-E-A-V-Y!"

Just at that moment, Warren entered. The hostess, who had been watching my encounter with the monk, screamed, "You were waiting for HIM?" in apparent total disbelief. "Banish these two to the boondocks," she ordered a conehead maitre-d' in a Star Wars costume with a sign "Be Kind to Aliens" on his back. As he led us to our table, I began to realize what Molly Murphy's was all about.

It's like walking onto someone's stage. Or going through the looking glass into wonderland. All the employees are not only in costumes, but in character. If a waitress has chosen to be a frog, for example, you'd better believe you will receive your drinking water tinted green and served with a "Rivett-Rivett!" If your waiter is named Blackbeard, as was ours, you will probably see him wave his cutlass in a loud argument with another waiter before the evening is through. The characters serving you at Molly Murphy's all write their own scripts as they go along. And an inverse version of Murphy's law pretty much applies. "If it can't happen, it will!"

Blackbeard seated us in high-back, flared Mandarin chairs at a table near a hut of bamboo and poker chips occupied by a young couple who looked as if they were dining elegantly in the jungle. I would not have been surprised to see them served by a cannibal because every table had its own characters waiting on it. Rasputin, Mr. Spock, Dracula, Charlie Chan, General Custer, Hot Lips Houlihan, Abe Lincoln and Batman are all to be found at Molly Murphy's. Bob Tayar, owner and developer of the unique Molly Murphy establishments in Tulsa and Oklahoma City (and more to come in Dallas and Denver) allows his employees to create their own characters and then play these characters to the hilt in a constant theater of innovation while rendering some of the sharpest and most dramatic dinner service anywhere. No two visits to Molly Murphy's are ever alike. One time you may be served by the Cowardly Lion and the next time it may be Bo-Peep.

It's obvious that the employees enjoy this arrangement too. They play their roles with real gusto and there must be more than a few present or potential actors among them. Though none of them have received the Academy Award, the restaurant has received the 1979 and 1980 Travel/Holiday Magazine recommendation as one of the outstanding restaurants of the world.

"Here's your menu," announced Blackbeard, unrolling a huge scroll. "I'll be back in three days." A short little tyke dressed as Raggedy Ann brought us our water in mason jars. The menu was imaginative too. It ranged from Chick-on-a-Stick to a Bacchus Feast for four or more, and offered much to tempt the palate on this trip into fantasy land. "Complaints," it warned, "should be made to our Public Relations Officer, Mr. Anthony 'Knuckles' Amato. Go to rear door in alley and ask for Knuckles."

"...the piece de resistance of Molly Murphy's service is the salad car. Yes, I said car, and it really is an automobile - a Jaguar in fact - with hot soup and salad makings set into the hood. Hovering over the Jaguar is a nervous character in pit mechanic's costume who watches for spills. He delight in hollering, "You dribbled salad dressing all over my salad car!" to timid souls with unsteady hands.

All in good fun, though, and everybody knows it. The place rocked with laughter as patrons became involved in the ongoing nonsense.

When a hard-hatted waiter dressed like the construction worker in the Village People delivered our bread, he proclaimed loudly, "Let us break bread together." He then proceeded to whack the towel-wrapped loaf of hot bread against the edge of the table to break off a portion for us.

Periodically, the entire retinue of costumed employees did a conga-line routine in and out among the tables singing something like "Fee, fie, fo, fum. The Bacchus Feast has just begun." They were led by several waiters bearing the dishes for the feast.

Obviously, Molly Murphy;s is not a place for the timid or the easily embarrassed. Beware the diner who asks the waiter or waitress where the rest rooms are. "Follow me," they will respond sweetly. Then as soon as the diner is on his feet, they chant "Potty Train! Potty Train! All aboard for the Potty Train" as others join in escorting the red-faced customer to the john.

You spend so much time laughing, you almost forget to notice the dandy decor. Funky is the work. Eclectic is another. The look changes every few feet. Bamboo huts, castle turrets, gazebos and other secluded nooks in which you will be anything but secluded once one of the characters discovers you, offer your choice of eccentric settings.

Don't look up. Something will appear ready to drop on you. You'll find everything from barrels to bookshelves and dinner plates hanging from the ceiling. Mirrored portholes add to the weird effect overhead and look like your escape hatches back into the real world.

But who would want to escape madcap, motley, raucous, ribald, wild and crazy Molly Murphy's? It's a total entertainment experience that changes with every visit. And after dinner, you can continue the evening dancing to the music of the times in the disco adjoining the main restaurant.

With all this atmosphere, you might wonder about the food. Let me assure you that over and above the entertainment and all the shenanigans you will find the food excellent. And where else in the world could you help yourself from a Jaguar salad car!"

That was the kind of advertising that can't be bought. You know those readers in Wisconsin would make it a point to come visit Molly Murphy's if they were ever anywhere near Oklahoma.

Through the years I have been told by a young mother that her baby was almost born there because just after placing their order for two prime rib dinners, she began having labor pains. Her hungry husband wouldn't leave until he had been served and had enjoyed his prime rib.

Another story came from an Edmond resident, who now owns an insurance agency. He took his prom date to Molly's before the prom, to find a big crowd congregated in the entry waiting to get into the disco, to wait to get into the dining room. He, thinking he was very suave, offered the podium girl, probably Polly Ester, a $5 dollar bill and asked for a table for two. She took the five dollars, waved it up in the air, and announced to all the people waiting that she had a $5 offer for a table, were there any higher bids? Of course there were many offers, but our staff was not allowed to accept money for a place in line. He was totally embarrassed…but what did he expect at Molly Murphy's? He realizes now how funny it was.

I have heard numerous stories of couples becoming engaged there but perhaps the story I remember most vividly is one that a young woman posted on the Molly Murphy website. Her parents would take her to Molly's when she was in grade school, and they had such a good time. Her parents later divorced and she said her best memories of her childhood are the happy times when she, her Mom and her Dad all went to Molly Murphy's and they were a family.

Management was not permitted to date staff members, but not only did our first General Manager, Hank, marry a beautiful, blonde, "Cub Scout," years later my own son married a beautiful blonde, "French Maid." Molly's kids had a good time and they made very good money in tips.

Bob and I weren't used to this kind of business where we didn't have to be there running things. In fact, when we went to Molly's for dinner, we simply assumed the role of customer, except we normally wouldn't want to take up a table by actually having dinner. We'd have cocktails, then stop by the Nomad II, where Jack Sussy was now selling his wonderful pizzas, to have dinner on the way home. Most every Saturday evening one would find Bob and me sitting in the front booth of the disco where Bob could keep an eye on the podium, the disco area and also see into the dining room. Bob would never dance and let the staff see him actually having fun, so I became quite a chair dancer.

Shortly after this grand opening of our restaurant we bought a lot in Nichols Hills, on the corner of Grand Boulevard and Pennsylvania, just across from the Oklahoma City Golf and Country Club. Our good friends were building a house next door. We paid $35,000 for that corner lot that in just a few years was worth $350,000. Raymond Carter was one of the best home designers in the area. His homes had been featured in Architectural Digest. After cutting out pictures in magazines of houses we liked we made an appointment with Raymond and he began designing our dream house.

It was a 7,200 square foot, Country French style house with four bedrooms and six bathrooms. I thought it amazing that I grew up without indoor plumbing when I was a child living on the farm at Byars, Oklahoma. It was about 1950 when we moved to Purcell that we actually had an indoor bathroom…and now I had six! It took about a year to build that house, but I had a wonderfully detailed set of plans to work from. With the help of a talented decorator, Pat, we were able to order all the furniture ahead of time so when the house was completed, we would be ready to move in with most everything we needed. Pat was young, blonde, and knew how to handle Bob, so he pretty much stayed out of the way and let us do what we wanted. I had saved money to purchase furniture and I soon figured out that by going to Dallas to the market center I could buy twice the amount of furniture as I could by paying retail. So, Pat and I made several day trips to Dallas to place our orders. What a thrill it was to be able to move into a new house with everything new. I mean everything! New cookware, new towels, new china, new linens…everything!

We moved into this house in the spring of 1978. We immediately felt at home. There were two boys across the street that were the same age as our son and attended the same school, Heritage Hall. Their parents were our age. Our friends, Buddy and Rhonda, lived next door, and another acquaintance lived two doors down. That made four of us couples who were all about the same age, three of us had children at Heritage Hall, and we were all very compatible. We also became good friends with another couple who lived in Quail Creek, and joked that they were our "token Quail Creekers." What good times we had together. On the three day weekends we would rotate the barbeque from house to house and each couple's circle of friends would become our friends.

The family next door was Lebanese and Bob had known Buddy for years. It was interesting that Bob never felt totally at easy with the Lebanese community OR the American community. He explained it this way: After his dad, Elias Tayar, died when Bob was nine years old, his mother had to run their grocery store and didn't have time to socialize with the people from the old country. Her children wanted to be American. They began going to The First Christian Church and they all married Americans so there simply were not many ties to the Lebanese community. But still, Bob was not American. He was well aware of being Arabic.

We were reminded of this when he thought we may want to become members of The Oklahoma City Golf and Country Club. We were told they had their quota of Jews and Arabs, so we never applied for membership.

Bob referred to the Nichols Hills crowd as the "blue-bloods." No one had ever heard of Bob and Jeffiee Tayar until we suddenly opened this crazy restaurant and built this fabulous house. Now people were very curious about us and our success. Well, we wanted to be part of this neighborhood so the summer we moved into it, I made invitations and had our son hand deliver them to the neighbors to come for an open house. I cooked all the food and spent days getting things ready. Looking back, I could have done much better, but it was my first attempt at entertaining at this level. The Friday Newspaper came and took pictures for their weekly edition of "The Beautiful People." They also published a story I wrote about the perils of building a new house. Gracious! We were becoming very social!

Living in the neighborhood that was referred to as home of "the beautiful people" we did all the requirements we felt necessary to fit into that category. Bob got rid of his Lebanese nose, bags under his eyes and the roll over his belt. I, too, was tucked, sucked, and siliconed. It all seemed to be the norm at that time.

When you have money, you are considered beautiful, smart, and in demand to serve on all sorts of boards and committees…and everyone would like to have you host their group in your home. It was after we lost our money that I realized this. I suddenly was NOT beautiful, smart or on anyone's guest list! But those "glory years" were unbelievable.

From 1978 until 1987 we opened our house to our church, our son's school, many charities, and of course, family. (Bob even served on the board of St. Elijah's Orthodox Church.) In 1980 I planned a family reunion for the Tayars. Bob had never been to a family reunion and didn't understand why I enjoyed going to my Golden's event every year. I decided it was time we plan a reunion for his family. Over a five day, 4th of July weekend, we had approximately 125 cousins, aunts, uncles, sisters, brothers, first cousins, second cousins..well, you get the idea, in and out of our house for the First (and only) Tayar Family Reunion. Bob arranged for a bartender to come from the restaurant as well as a couple of cocktail waitresses to serve us. I had three ladies working in the kitchen to help serve and clean. One evening we had a barbeque dinner catered by the pool and were entertained by a bluegrass band. All the Lebanese ladies cooked one big meal of Yebra, Kibba, Talamies, Taboulie, every Lebanese dish imaginable. All of our bedrooms were full, and I rented a tent and cots to set up on the side of the house for all the children. They especially enjoyed it when the sprinklers came on at 6 a.m.! I served continental breakfasts and all the relatives who were staying at motels would join us for the entire day and evening. Our large drive looked like we must be having the Mother of all Parties since it was full for five days. The last evening a cute young couple, seeing all the cars, thought they could crash the party, not knowing it was a family reunion. It was apparent they were party crashers because when they walked in the house, they were the only blue eyed, blondes there. Everyone knew they weren't relatives.

We also entertained celebrities and political figures at both Molly's and in our home. Frank Keating and his then young family were weekend guests, and Sen. David Boren was once a guest when we hosted a party for the O U Medical Center. It was a fundraiser and Sen. Boren's cousin, singer and songwriter, Hoyt

Axton, "(Joy to The World)," was the special guest. I was thrilled to actually meet Hoyt and play hostess to him because I had been a long time fan of his.

Jeffiee standing, Hoyt Axton, and friends.

Tanya Tucker would stop by the restaurant every time she played in Oklahoma City. Tanya would go back into the kitchen and visit with the staff there as well as the front end characters. Ron Howard came with his wife, back when he still had hair. Tennessee Ernie Ford entertained the other diners as much as our waiters by wrapping a cloth dinner napkin around his head and greeting folks in all the booths around him. TV personality Sarah Purcell came and brought her crew to film the restaurant for "Real People," a new TV show. The BBC also filmed for a documentary, but it was Playboy's article that really gave us national recognition, and we were the recipient of the Holiday Fine Dining Award for several years.

Ron Howard, his wife, and Donny Most
having dinner at Molly's

During this period I was able to drive back to Ardmore and shop at the Jean-Lee Dress Shop. It had been an exclusive shop for probably 30 years. When I lived in Ardmore, I couldn't afford to shop there, except for the one dress I bought for graduation, but now I could go and take my Nichols Hills friends. We would come home on a shopping high that was better than any drug could possibly be. Everywhere I wore those expensive, beautiful outfits I would get compliments.

Then there was the jewelry. On our 20th anniversary Bob gave me a 3.25 diamond that I had always wanted in order to keep up with my new status. And the furs. A couple of jackets and a black, full-length mink coat. And the new Cadillac every couple of years.

There were the trips. Summers I would drive to California with our son and Bob would fly there and meet us. We stayed at Newport Beach, then Malibu, and finally our neighbors were able to get us into the exclusive La Jolla Beach and Tennis Club. For several summers that was our family vacation. But there were also the ski and gambling trips to Lake Tahoe. There were several Las Vegas junkets, one to Aruba, a few trips to Mexico and my favorite was our family trip to New York City. We stayed at the Plaza Hotel and rented a limousine to drive us to all the tourist sites. We attended a Broadway show every evening, but on the final night we were there I sent our son back to Oklahoma City to spend the night with his aunt and uncle because I didn't want to warp his sweet mind. We were going to see " The Best Little Whorehouse in Texas." I didn't think it was appropriate for him to see. I had no idea it was just a musical comedy. At his age, I'm sure he had sneaked a peek at a Playboy, but I wasn't taking any chances.

I became active in the Daughters of the American Revolution, after proving I was descended from patriots of the Revolutionary War. I did this because my maiden name was Golden. That sounds slightly Jewish. When we were dating, Bob would introduce me to his Lebanese friends saying, "This is Jeffiee Golden; she's not a Jew." Well, I didn't know exactly what that meant so I began some genealogical researching to see just what my ancestry happened to be. That is when I discovered that I was eligible for the DAR. Bob was right - I was not a Jew.

My house was the site of many meetings for the DAR as well as other lineage societies, patriotic groups, and book clubs. For a week in April, I would join other DAR members in Washington, D.C., for the annual Continental Congress. My friend and I didn't stay at the less expensive hotels as the other members from Oklahoma would do. We stayed at the J.W. Marriott usually and had a first class trip. I also served as Chapter Regent and a State Officer during that time, as well as holding a couple of National Committee Chairmanships.

During these years we were able to send our son to Europe for one summer with a group from Brown University. We could afford to keep him in a private school. We also built another Molly Murphy's House of Fine Repute in Tulsa. We remodeled Bonaparte's Drive-In to a Sweet Peas Family Restaurant. Bob was having a new concept designed called, "Ta'Molly's Mexican Restaurant and Cantina." Everything Bob touched turned to gold. The Daily Oklahoman wrote a nice article about him and his successes. We were at the top and had achieved more than I had ever dreamed. I had everything…the beautiful house, the new car, the clothes, the jewelry, the trips - so why did I cry every time I heard Willie Nelson sing "You Were Always on My Mind?"

Part III

Losin' It

Ta'Molly's Mexican Restaurant was a beautiful building, inside and out, having been designed by a California girl who was tall, thin, blonde, and younger than me. (But I liked her, anyway.) She designed colorful uniforms for the staff and left no detail undone. Bob hired a chef from a well known Mexican restaurant in Dallas and brought in his nephew who had just graduated Stanford University to be our General Manager. Once again we had a Grand Opening with all the festivities in the spring of 1982. But something didn't feel right to me. The night before we had this Grand Opening I was home alone and decided to go to the mall and window shop. There was an amethyst and diamond ring that caught my eye and though I am not an impulse buyer, I bought that ring. There was a feeling that the money was being spent too fast, and it wouldn't be there much longer...but jewelry will last. So I bought the ring.

Our 20th wedding anniversary fell shortly after opening Ta Molly's. Bob and I were having lunch with the corporate staff and the restaurant manager when someone happened to mention that it was our anniversary. Bob, thinking he was being funny told everyone that Jeffiee had been married for 20 years but HE had not. I ignored that stupid joke, held up my new amethyst and diamond ring, and very sweetly said, "And Bob, I want to thank you for this beautiful anniversary gift." Not much he could say after that. Those times he would think he was being cute and say things that were unflattering to me in front of people, I would smile and say to them that Bob and I have an agreement. He gets to talk big in front of people and I get to shop!

From the time we opened Molly Murphy's in Oklahoma City, I was no longer a part of the operations of the business. My role was mom, homemaker, and volunteer. Hank Kraft did such a terrific job with the opening of the Molly's in Tulsa and the changing of Bonaparte's Drive In to Sweet Peas that I didn't worry about things at the corporate offices. Hank left before Ta'Molly's opened. I wasn't included in the decision making any longer and it seems there was no one who would say "no" to Bob. His ego was getting bigger and bigger.

He decided he wanted the ceiling and walls in the kitchen at this Mexican restaurant to be ceramic tile, so they could be hosed down easily for cleaning. That is a nice thing to have in an area where there is a lot of grease, from frying tortillas, but it is also quite expensive, to the tune of about $400,000. Of course, the tall, thin, blonde, younger than me designer agreed it would be great to have a ceramic-tiled kitchen since her fee was a percentage of the cost of the building. Bob had put up other property we had acquired as collateral for the bank loan to build this new restaurant. But when he asked for the $400,000, for a ceramic tiled kitchen, Liberty Bank wanted more collateral. They asked him to put our house up, assuring Bob they didn't want to take the house, but it would just make the loan tidier. Bob made some very good business deals, but this wasn't one of them. We signed over our house as collateral for that ceramic tiled kitchen. This house that we only owed $220,000 on, that now appraised for $1.1 million. We signed our house over as collateral...for a ceramic tiled kitchen. I was beginning not to like that tall, thin, blonde, younger than me designer.

On the opening day we had a ribbon cutting ceremony in front of Ta'Molly's with the newspaper there to take a picture for the business section of The Daily Oklahoman. Bob, his nephew who was the General Manager, the designer, and a few others stood for the photo, but I wasn't asked to join them. At the last minute, the nephew turned to me and said, "Come on, Aunt Jeffiee, you need to be in this picture." So I was. But Bob had forgotten about me.

Ta'Molly's opening 1982

That first summer Ta'Molly's was opened, Bob owned an Excalibur, well, actually, he owned two of those cars. The Excalibur Corporation was based in Milwaukee and owned by the family that had built Studebakers in the '50s. Our first Excalibur was crème and maroon and looked like the "Chitty Chitty Bang Bang" car. It had a trunk attached behind it and chrome pipes on the front. Our salad car at the Tulsa Molly's was the frame of this exact model. Our other Excalibur was brown and very elegant looking, being styled after the Duesenberg. They were both eye catchers.

Between these two cars, my Seville, our son's Bronco, and the race car, we had a couple of hundred thousand dollars sitting in our garage.

The race car...well, at the age of 50, Bob decided to take up racing. He and Paul Newman. Bob raced a Formula 440 at Hallett near Tulsa and in the states surrounding Oklahoma. Now Bob wasn't a mechanic and had no intention of getting his hands dirty, so he hired a mechanic who would pull this car to all the races behind his motor home. The mechanic and his wife would camp with the other racers at the site but Bob and I would find the nicest hotel nearby and stay there. At Hallet we would drive to Tulsa and stay at The Williams Plaza and have dinner at our own restaurant. Bob won Rookie of the Year but gave up that hobby when a younger driver crashed and was left paralyzed from the neck down. That scared Bob enough to make him give up that racing dream.

Back to that summer we opened Ta'Molly's. Bob had several parking places marked "handicapped" near the front door. He decided one of those spots was for him but he thought if he marked it "Bob Tayar," people would resent it, so he just kept it marked "handicapped" and parked there. I hated pulling up and parking there in one of the Excaliburs while customers were walking into the restaurant. It was such a blatant display of affluence I didn't even want to get out of the car.

This $2 million restaurant was opened three months before Penn Square Bank closed, and we Oklahomans who are old enough remember what that started. It was the oil bust, but no one realized exactly what was happening at the time. It took a couple of years for the realization to hit us. Ta'Molly's opened up doing a very good business, but it began to drop. Bob hired a consultant to tell us what was wrong, and the consultant couldn't find anything wrong. The customers loved the place. He polled them as they left. The problem was that Oklahoma was in a recession. Molly Murphy's wasn't affected, however, because we had plenty of out of state customers during the week, and on the weekends it was still a place of celebration for local residents. Bob remodeled Ta'Molly's changing the name to "Bobby Lee's" but that made no difference in business nor did his changing Sweet Peas to "Gump's." The only difference is that the $400,000 trust account for our son was lost on the remodeling expenses.

One thing that did change though was my status in the business. Without being invited I simply went back to work in the corporate offices. Our son was in college at Oklahoma University, and I had plenty of time. Lord, what a surprise I had when I tried to open the check books to look at the balances. First, there were no real check books. Everything was being done on the computer, and I had never been part of that change. When I did our accounts payable, I simply had a check book for each of the two Bonaparte's restaurants and I wrote all the checks by hand to pay the bills. Then our bookkeeper, Rae, would do whatever it was that she had to do. I knew in my head how much each operating account, each payroll account and each tax account held as a balance. If I forgot, I could open up the ledger sized check book and just look at it. Not so now. There was a man called a controller, who did everything on the computer, and I was at his mercy to be able to find out numbers. But I could tell that 2+2=4, and we were only coming up with 3. I looked around the offices and saw that we had this controller, a payroll clerk, Bob's personal secretary, and a couple of other people that I never could tell exactly what they did working in this beautiful condominium office. After learning how to get into the books, I would go to the office at 5 a.m. to study through things and see just where we were and how much we owed. If I waited until 9 a.m. the creditors would be calling and at least twice a day I would be in tears from their ugly demands for payment. Bob would isolate himself in his plush office and try to figure out how to pull us out of this situation. He couldn't believe all he had built up was about to fall.

I was trying to cut costs and the corporate office seemed unnecessary and a drain on each restaurant for their part of its support. We were making a $3,500 a month payment to Wells Fargo for this condominium office when we could simply rent space across the street for $750 a month. OK. But there was no way to get out of this payment to Wells Fargo. We had to stop paying them, so we did. Oh, of course, they sued us. In fact, they needed to serve Bob papers to get him into court, and they had a very difficult time. They couldn't get to him in our house in Nichols Hills because it had a security system that wouldn't let anyone in that we didn't want there. They tried to serve him at the office, but there were enough people up front that the server could never get by them. But one day I knew a process server was waiting to catch Bob as he left the office. Bob needed to leave but there was no way he could without being seen. I phoned a friend who had a blonde wig, Dolly Parton style, and asked her to bring it to the office. She did, and also a trench coat. We put that wig on Bob, tied the trench coat loosely around him, and I drove the car up next to the door, he jumped in and off we drove. I don't know how long that server waited in the parking lot.

The controller told me he felt our main problem was Bob's ego. That was probably true, but I also felt part of that problem was a controller being paid $60,000 a year and not controlling anything. I suggested we let the $60,000 controller go. My thoughts were that he let us get into a mess, and it cost us $60,000 a year. I could let us get in that mess for free. So I became the controller without even knowing what it was a controller did. We moved our offices across the street, released all the staff and hired Sue, an old fashioned bookkeeper. She and I got along famously! She understood how to cut costs in the office. We backed down to just the two Molly Murphy's, one in Oklahoma City and one in Tulsa. The Tulsa store cleared about $30,000 a year, much less than the Oklahoma City store, but it was doing fine and paying for the property it stood on. We were sued by many creditors in those mid-'80s wanting payment for money Ta'Molly's owed. Many large companies, including restaurants, were filing Chapter 11 Bankruptcy, but Bob refused to do that. He still had dreams of expanding Molly Murphy's and Ta'Molly's out of state. He was afraid a Bankruptcy would stifle any expansion plans. So we set up payments with Molly's paying the bills for all the losses.

This arrangement was working out until Liberty Bank called their note. They wanted $2 million plus the 22% interest being charged during that time. We sold the property Ta'Molly's stood on and the lot we owned next door. We sold the property in Tulsa that Molly's stood on and the lot next door with all the proceeds going to Liberty Bank. But that wasn't enough. They wanted our house. We hated to give it up but, you know, it wasn't fun any longer when we couldn't afford to live there. It would have been nice if the bank would have let us sell it and keep enough to buy something smaller but they didn't.

Bankers were difficult to deal with during these "oil bust" days. They acted as though they were working with us to get all these creditors off our backs and ran up $50,000 in legal fees for us, then, when things were under control, they stepped in and demanded our house. We were left owing a law firm that I refer to as "Kick and Chain Me," (Kirk and Chaney) the $50,000. Liberty had led us to believe they would help with that, but they didn't. Kick and Chain Me made me take all my jewelry and fur coats downtown to have them appraised as though they were going to take them away from me. We came up with a payment plan to get them out of our lives, but they sure made ours miserable for a long time and I still have bad feelings for them. But guess what happened to me. I quit crying. Willie could sing any song he pleased and couldn't get a tear from me because I was too busy fighting the piranhas.

And I was busy finding a place to live. Liberty Bank allowed us to have one last Christmas in our Big House, as I had come to call it. Our neighbors owned a condo at The Waterford and we were able to rent it for $1,800 a month. Bob didn't want to sign a lease because being the eternal optimist, he thought we would be building again in Nichols Hills very soon.

His plan was to get an investor to build a Molly's in California, so in January of 1987, when the moving van arrived, with eight inches of snow on the ground, I was there alone to greet them. My sister helped me with the estate sale after the movers were done. Bob arranged this meeting with investors so he wouldn't have to be part of this move because he just couldn't bear to leave this house...the symbol of his success. It wasn't exactly fun for me either but I didn't feel I had the luxury to whine. Plus, I was trying to keep up a front for my DAR friends and the community by saying that since our son was living in Norman and a student at OU, we simply wanted to downsize from the 7200 -squarefoot house and would live at The Waterford. The Waterford wasn't exactly shabby. Molly's still provided a very good cash flow and our lifestyle wasn't that different. In fact, the next winter when our son was an escort at the Bachelor Club's Debutante Ball, and Bob was dressed in his custom made tuxedo, and I in my Jean-Lee formal gown, with my mink coat and jewelry, as we got into his Mercedes, I blurted out, "It's funny. We don't look poor!"

Bob & Jeffiee with Pres. Bush

Our life continued not on such a grand scale but it was hard to feel sorry for us. For me, it was great to be back a part of the business. We seemed to have things under control, and we were meeting our financial obligations. When our friends decided to sell the condo in 1990, we found a lovely house in The Greens that, after I cashed our last IRAs and did some remodeling, was sort of a mini-Nichols Hills house. All the living areas looked out back to a pool and my ebony, baby grand Steinway piano gave a lot of class to that house.

Our son graduated from OU to become the General Manager at Molly's. That was when I decided it was my turn to go to school, so I did and earned an Associate Degree in Business Management from Oklahoma City Community College.

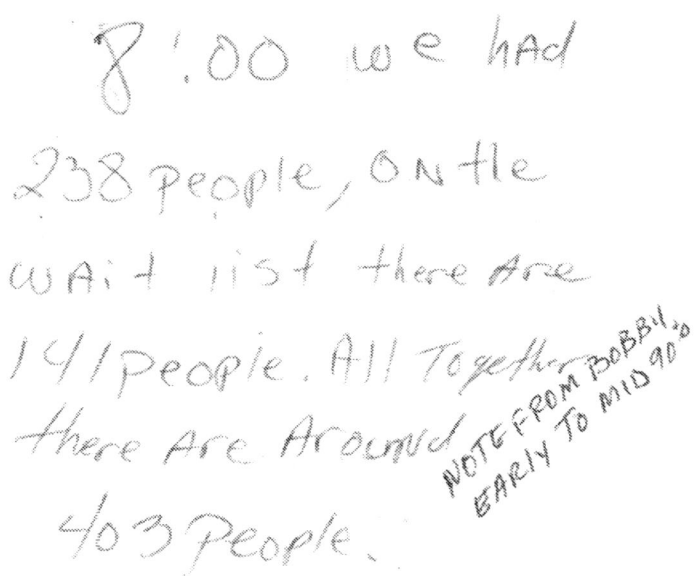

Bobby's customer count written on a cocktail napkin
for his Dad to see how business was that evening...ca 1993

Bob continued to try to expand the restaurant out of state. He
actually found several investors but never enough to meet the necessary cost of land, building, and equipment. He also found a man
in Dallas who took our business public, which Bob thought was our
way to expansion. Not so. This Dallas man was a white collar
crook who made $250,000 from our stock and left us with all the
legal fees to rescind his scheme.

Still trying to hit on something to make money, Bob took the
cash we had saved and put in a couple of restaurants that were
really bad ideas. One was called Goin' Bananas in a Texas mall
and the other was Tijuana Tillie's at Quail Springs Mall. Seems his
golden touch was gone. We had to close those places within a few
months and were left with debt that once again, Molly Murphy's
had to assume. I could tell he was losing his confidence.

Then there was the Oklahoma City bombing in 1995. That
was such a disaster no one was in the mood for a fun, festive dinner for months! It happened in April, which was the beginning of

our good season for business.   The spring was when horse shows began at the fair grounds, proms were held, and events were scheduled that drew people in to Oklahoma City from smaller towns nearby. We simply had no good season that year. When we were already depleted of cash reserves from our reluctance to file bankruptcy during the oil bust of the '80s, and from the loss of those futile attempts to open new restaurants, there was no money to carry us through these months of meager revenue. For the previous 19 years the summer business carried us through the winter's slow business. It was something we could count on.

Bob's brother, who had loaned us that $3,000 to get into business years ago, died. His widow wanted to move to an apartment and sell their house but was unable to find a buyer. Although the house had been neglected for several years and wasn't very attractive, my son always thought it was cozy. Realizing we were getting in a bad financial situation, we sold our house in The Greens and moved into this neglected house. After I did some remodeling, it was really quite pretty. Of course, my beautiful furniture made anyplace look good, but I did sell that baby grand piano and the replica antique billiard table to cover a payroll, but there wasn't room for them anyway in this smaller house.

Before we moved from The Greens, our son married the "French Maid" who worked at Molly's. I had a premonition this wedding was my last hurrah, and I wanted things to be as nice and fun as possible, so I didn't mind spending the last of our savings. We took all the out of town relatives to the restaurant for dinner on the Friday evening of the wedding weekend, with everyone having a wonderful time. Saturday morning, after the rehearsal at St. Elijah's Orthodox Church, I had brunch at our house around the pool. I did the cooking but had someone to help serve and mix drinks. That evening I had a Lebanese dinner for all the extended family...probably 40 to 50 people. Then Sunday evening was the wedding. We had two bands play at The Greens Country Club for the reception dinner; one American and one Arabic. We did the Arabic folk dances with Cousin Kenneth leading the parade carrying the traditional Kibba, a meat and wheat dish that is traditionally served at Arabic weddings, through the rooms before serving it. Bobby and his new bride, Kara, looked like Ken and Barbie. All those years of private school, the summer in Europe, the fraternity, the Bachelor's Club, had turned our son into a very charming, well mannered young man.

Once Bobby married, it was difficult for his dad to control his life. Wives resent that. There was friction between father and son, and one day Bobby stormed out of the corporate office saying he quit as General Manager. A couple of days later he phoned his dad to see if they were still going to the Dallas Cowboys ball game. Bob said, "I thought you didn't like me anymore." Bobby was very mature. He replied, "Dad, I don't like to work for you, but you're still my Dad." So they went to the ball game. But Bob never got over his son leaving his employment.

So, Bob was left to be the GM. And we all knew this wasn't good. We moved out of our rented corporate offices and began to office in the back room of the restaurant. Bob was not happy about our financial situation. He was not happy his son wasn't there. He was not happy that I was beginning to run things. I never wanted to run things. Everything I knew about business, I learned from him. I just wanted him to step up and be the man I married. I wanted Bob to come up with a great idea as he had in the past to create more business. And I wanted to be there to help him.

I remember the day the agent from the Oklahoma Tax Commission came to the restaurant to post a lien on the front door. He was nice enough to let us cover it with a menu, but that was the final step. We had no choice but to file Chapter 11, reorganization. I was glad Bob finally agreed to do this, but the fact is he had no choice. We met with an attorney and took the necessary steps to get things moving and hold creditors off until we could get this action filed. Interestingly, Bob felt great relief after taking this dreaded move. This was the fall of 1995.

It was during this time that a local meat company had a judgment against us for debt, but we had set up an agreement to make monthly payments. They apparently got wind of our Chapter 11 filing so they sent two men from the Sheriff's Department out to clear the cash register on a Saturday night. They arrived about midnight but...surprise...there was no money in the cash register. Each waiter acted as his own bank. It wasn't until the end of the evening when the waiters closed out their checks and settled their tip pool that there was any cash in the till. The two Sheriffs waited. Bob had already come home and gone to bed by this time so it was the closing waiter who phoned us about 1 a.m. to tell us what was happening. The money owed us on credit cards was safe but the cash could be taken. I needed this cash because we had just written payroll that day, knowing the checks wouldn't be cashed until after this Saturday night's business proceeds were deposited in the bank on Monday morning. I was becoming adept at juggling. Therefore, the realization that there would be no cash to cover that payroll made me hysterical. Bob went back to sleep but I jumped into jeans and sweatshirt, without bothering to don underwear, and high-tailed it down to Molly's.

When I walked into the office there was all the cash, about $4,000 stacked on the desk. I just began to grab it, stuffing it in my handbag, when suddenly my arms were twisted behind my back and I was handcuffed. I was taken to jail. I don't recall the charge, but the charge didn't really matter. My wrists hurt. The sky was falling. Payroll would bounce.

When a person is arrested they are fingerprinted, their picture is taken, and they are locked in a cell. I had two other women as roommates. One was there because she and her boyfriend had a fight. She called the police, and they were both arrested. She was furious about that. I just sat listening to the two of them and pretended I was someplace else. Soon Bob came to take me home. The next Monday I took my old Cadillac by the bank and asked for a loan against it for $4,000 to cover the payroll checks that would be coming in that day.

After we filed Chapter 11, creditors were a little bit nicer to us because they realized we had been "slow pay" because we didn't have the money. Apparently they thought we just didn't want to pay before. Well, Bob had an arrogance about him that put many people off. He always drove a flashy car, whether it was an Excalibur, Mercedes, Porsche, or BMW.

November of that year was not a good month for us. Bob had a brother who died, and my oldest sister died. And then there was "The Incident".

Part IV

The Incident

Every time I would say to myself, well, it can't get any worse, it would. When "The Incident" occurred you must understand Bob's emotional state so you may appreciate why he reacted as he did. First, his son had left the family business. Second, we had lost both our Big House in Nichols Hills and our smaller house in The Greens and were renting his older brother's house. Third, the April bombing of the Murrah Building had ruined our business for our season, and we had filed Chapter 11, which he had avoided for the past ten years. Yes, he felt a relief after having taking this legal action to keep creditors at bay, but he still viewed it as giving up.

Everyone knew Bob wasn't good with the public. He would never have been acting General Manager if there had been enough revenue to hire someone capable to replace our son. So that is when those two women each won their $25 gift certificates by phoning into a radio show and being the 10th caller. The person at the station should have explained they could only use "one per party per visit," because they certainly had been told. We didn't want the salesman to bring all his friends out for a free party. This policy was NOT printed on the gift certificates because these were the same certificates we sold. So, the ones given away for promotions were stamped with large red letters, COMP. We hoped with this policy of using one per party per visit, that paying customers would accompany the free dinner recipient so we would not have a total loss. This is not unusual in the restaurant business.

Cindy Trent and Debbie Pester had both won these Free Dinner at Molly Murphy's $25 gift certificates, with COMP stamped
on the front in bold red letters. They came bringing them and a
third person for dinner in November,1995. Their total bill was not
much more than $50 because they ordered the least expensive
items on the menu and nothing from the bar. So, when Gypsy, their
server, presented their bill for about $35, they didn't expect to pay
but somewhere in the neighborhood of $10. Gypsy explained to
them they could use the other gift certificate another time, but they
weren't happy with that and asked for the manager. Bob Tayar was
definitely not a public relations person. He told them, as nicely as
he could, they could not use the second gift certificate that night
but could another night. A public relations person would have said
OK...no problem, but as I said, Bob was not a public relations person. Well, Ms. Pester was pissed! She said something to the effect
that if they had known they would have to pay, they wouldn't have
come. Bob told them we didn't need that kind of business and
showed them the door.

A day or so later one of the ladies phoned the restaurant, and
I was the person to answer. I listened to her complaint but it was
the first I had heard of this. Knowing nothing about it, I told her I
would have to check into the matter. When Bob arrived at the
office, I asked him about this complaint and he was not about to do
anything other than what he had told them...they could use the
other gift certificate on another visit. When the woman phoned
back she used some pretty ugly words, so I just hung up on her.

Apparently she called our NBC affiliate's KFOR's, "In Your
Corner" with Brad Edwards to lodge her complaint against Molly
Murphy's. Brad Edwards was a nice guy, but he was not at work
that day. A reporter, Anthony Foster, took the information, and it
must have been a slow news day at the station because it seemed to
me they spent much more time on this than was warranted by her
complaint.

The first thing that happened at about 4 p.m. was a call to
Molly's that I answered. Anthony Foster told me who he was and
that he would like a comment or an interview about this incident.
I told him we had nothing to say but he was persistent in his
demand for a statement. Since that office was so small, Bob could

overhear my part of the conversation and told me to hang up the phone. I did. Well, he just phoned back. On this second phone call I said, "Mr. Foster, we have nothing to say." (He recorded this statement and played it on their newscast.) He said he wanted to speak with a manager. Unbeknownst to him, he was speaking with an owner, but he wanted a manager so I had Bob pick up the other phone. Bob just put it on speaker so I could hear everything said. The conversation went something like this:

> Bob: I told you already I am not giving an interview and quit calling here.
>
> Anthony Foster: If you don't give me what I need over the phone I will come there with my camera and get the interview.
>
> Bob: Slam...hangs up the phone.

Bob then phoned the secretary to the manager at the TV station, Ann Evick. He knew her from The Greens Golf Course so he felt comfortable asking her what was going on and why Foster was so determined to get an interview. Bob knew no one had a legal obligation to give an interview on TV or radio if they chose not to do so. Ann knew nothing about Foster's calls but said she would tell the manager as soon as he came out of his meeting. Bob and I thought it was over.

Not so. Foster phoned back a third time and said he was on his way for an interview unless Bob wanted to do it over the phone. Bob, the hot tempered Arab, warned Foster if he set one foot on our property, he would find his ass in the parking lot, and he should check with his manager before he drove out to Molly's. Foster said he had talked with his manager, and his manager said to go for it. Bob slammed down the phone again. He called Ann back a second time. Seems Ann's manager was still in that meeting so she hadn't discussed it with him yet. Well, it was getting close to 5 p.m. and for me, it was quittin' time so I went home.

It was about 5:15 that I got the call from Bob saying I would never believe what had just happened. He had just opened for business with customers already in the dining room when the girl from the podium, Genie, I believe, came to find him saying someone was in the entrance with a TV camera asking for the manager. Bob looked over and saw Anthony Foster standing near the podium with a microphone in his hand and next to him was his camera man, Brad Riggin, with his camera rollin'. Well, you can imagine how that would affect a person who had specifically said he did not want to give an interview and the reporter was not to come to his property. Remember, this is public property only for the purpose of dining and dancing, not public for conducting TV interviews. Bob could have had the two of them arrested for trespassing. Of course, he wasn't told this until afterward and at the time this was happening, he was so angry he wouldn't have thought of it anyway. He began walking toward the two men and 17 times, yes, 17 times (we counted them during the trial when the video was shown on slow play) told them to get off the property. But did they turn to leave? No. So by the time Bob got to them he began pushing Foster out the door and there was that camera within inches of his face, so he pushed that camera, too. Now picture this: Bob Tayar was in his mid-60s at this time, 5'10" tall, white hair, very thin, pushing Anthony Foster, in his 30s, about 6'4", weighing well over 200 pounds, out the door. Do you really think Bob hurt him?

This is what Bob relayed to me as having occurred, but if I didn't believe him, there would always be the video Brad Riggin was taping to prove what happened. Bob said he reacted like a crazy man and was certain they would show it on the news. We sure didn't need this kind of publicity, especially after we had just filed Chapter 11, and had come up with a plan to get things back on track by the next spring. Geez! Was there ever an end to all this crap?

I phoned KFOR's news department to try to convince them not to air this damaging video. I got a Melissa Klinzing, news director, on the line. I asked, then begged her not to show this on the news. It didn't seem newsworthy and since we had just filed Chapter 11, it would not be good for us or our business. At the end of the conversation, she said, "We didn't have a story until your husband touched our news reporter. Now we have a story and we're going with it." Oh, my God. I knew I couldn't persuade her to change her mind so I hung up.

I phoned Molly's to report this to Bob, when the head waiter, "Karate Kid," told me Foster had called the police to come watch as Foster placed Bob under citizen's arrest, then the police handcuffed Bob, pushed his head down and put him in the back seat of their police car to take him to jail for Assault and Battery charges. And of course, Brad Riggin, cameraman for KFOR, was there to film it all.

I opened the Yellow Pages to find a bondsman who would get Bob out of jail. I spoke with several, and it seemed none of them had anything good to say about KFOR's news. The one I selected actually said they would do it for free. Next, I contacted the attorney handling our bankruptcy to see if he had any ideas. While we were talking he told me to turn on Channel 4's news. They were already starting teasers for their 10 p.m. newscast about a popular restaurateur attacking a KFOR reporter, or some such garbage. I phoned our son to warn him about this newscast so he wouldn't be shocked, as well as my sister and my mother. I uncorked a bottle of wine and by the time the 10 o'clock news came on, that bottle was empty. It wasn't the wine that made me feel sick to my stomach. It was what I saw on TV. Yes, Bob did look like a crazy man pushing Foster and the camera. His face was distorted with anger and I was glad I wasn't on the other end of this outburst. The thing that kept going through my mind was that I couldn't keep up any sort of image any longer. I would simply have to leave town. Things were happening that were beyond my control and I had to leave.

Bob was released from jail by the time the midnight newscast aired, so he was home with me watching it. Nothing had changed from the earlier newscast. It didn't get any better. There are no words to describe our anguish. My stomach churned and I felt sick. Finally I dozed off to sleep a little but Bob sat in his recliner all night and we both watched again on the 6:30 a.m. newscast. Again, it had not gotten any better.

After realizing the nightmare was real, I decided I should carry on as usual so I put on my leotard and drove to my aerobics class. What a shock to start the car; turn on the radio, to hear that Molly Murphy's and my husband were the topic of conversation. I changed stations. Same thing. On three different stations we were being trashed by callers who only knew what they saw on TV that was so damaging to us. None of them knew what really happened so the minute I arrived at All American Fitness Center, I borrowed the phone and called one of the morning show hosts to give the true account of what happened. My heart was pounding because I wasn't used to being on the air but I tried to explain The Incident as it really happened. Then I went on to my class.

When I opened the door to the low impact aerobic classroom, all conversation stopped. There was silence as I walked over the wood plank floor to my regular spot. Finally the woman next to me said, "We didn't expect you here this morning. We thought you would be getting your husband out of jail." My stomach began to churn once again and it was all I could do to hold back from telling her she didn't know what she was talking about and maybe she was a stupid bitch. But it seemed everyone in the room had suddenly become stupid bitches, so I stayed quiet. As soon as our class was over, I rushed out of there.

After going home and changing clothes, I stopped by the bank to pick up our opening cash bag and make the last night's deposit. Normally the tellers would speak and joke while I waited for my deposit to be counted. This morning everyone seemed to be quite busy because not a soul looked up as I entered the lobby. However, as I was leaving, one sweet girl who sat by the exit said she heard me on the radio. Suddenly getting to the restaurant could wait. I had to tell this girl, in detail, about The Incident.

It was about noon when I did get to the office to find the phones constantly ringing. There were three reasons for all these phone calls: one was to cancel their Christmas party reservations, another to say they supported Bob and they were tired of this kind of news reporting, (KFOR had several of these expose newscasts prior to Molly's) and finally, and mostly, the callers who talked so mean and ugly to me. It seemed every person who had been released from employment at any of the restaurants during the 35 years we had been in business decided to call and vent their anger at us. They said dreadful things about Bob. All the people who had less than perfect service or less than perfect food must have also called. And even one woman phoned who didn't like Bob because she saw him park in the handicapped parking space.

These were the hardest days we'd ever had in business. We needed to keep things running but Bob was feeling such hatred towards himself, it was very difficult. The newscast and radio talk shows continued for several days. It just didn't stop.

On November 30, 1995, there was an article in The Midwest City Sun, a local newspaper, written by Dick Hefton. That article was a small ray of hope for us. It was written after hearing our side of the story when I phoned the radio station the morning after The Incident.

Here is how it read:

"As if being singled out by a grand jury for unprofessionalism wasn't enough, KFOR Channel 4 sends its version of a SWAT team out to make a raid on a trendy restaurant with a flimsy charge launched by some disgruntled customer. Actually, it really wasn't even a paying customer that put on the hunt one night this week with no less than Anthony Foster, the station's answer to a stealth bomber.

No. It was a pair of unhappy customers who both tried to cash but were rebuffed two $25 coupons handed out free by some radio station. Incensed that the owners of Molly Murphy's out on S. Meridian refused to honor but one freebie at a time, they took their case, not to some official authority, but to the local television outlet known for trying to gain audience by embarrassing local businesses - KFOR.

Now, as the world waits anxiously while our troops are prime for a march into harms way, off goes Superman to protect our free society from the menacing manager of Molly Murphy's House of Fine Repute," as its slogan claims.

So picture a full-dress raid crashing into your front door. The imposing figure of the stealth investigator backed up by commandos armed with ominous-looking weapons hidden behind blinding strobe lights is enough to scare Bond, James Bond.

Is it a stick-up? No. The team is uniformly decked out in black slickers.

Is it an FBI or ATF dope raid? No. Those official-looking yellow Day-Glo letters don't spell FBI, ATF, Po-lice or Sheriff. More scary than any of those, they read "K-F-O-R!"

Unfortunately, KFOR apparently has little else to keep its ratings alive than to bait, antagonize, bully and badger owner Bob Tayar until Tayar does exactly what they hope he will do.

After asking them to leave his property, ordering them to leave his property, then pushing the giant Foster, who is twice

Tayar's size, out the door, Tayar smashes one of the cameras and punches Foster out.

Now, believe this. Foster files a complaint then brings the camera back to film Tayar being cuffed and taken to jail to be booked.

Foster and KFOR demonstrated they have nothing of more importance to fill air time. But our law enforcement officers especially this time of year are hard pressed to give the protection our community needs. The don't have time to chase around playing games with frivolous setups by rating hungry media.

KFOR should at least have to pay the cost of such trivialities. Yelling "wolf" in a crowded theatre or getting caught making crank calls is no worse than the silliness resorted to by Foster and his merry marauders. Perhaps the grand jury, which is still in session, might want to take another look at this media waste.

Or, maybe with this latest example they can just "rest their case."

That article was with me constantly for the next several months just so I could read it and remember we weren't the bad guys.

Bob thought we should sue KFOR, dba Palmer Communications. This may be a good time to explain that KFOR today, in 2007, is not the same as it was in 1995. At that time Palmer Communications owned the station and hired the News Director, Melissa Klinzing, to help get them in the #1 news spot locally. November is a special month for television viewers. It is Sweeps month. This means the higher the viewing audience on the Nielsen ratings, the more a station can charge advertisers. Also, the more valuable that station becomes, and this was important to KFOR in 1995. They wanted to sell and they did. Time Warner purchased that station, I heard, for about $33 million. So, KFOR today is not managed as it was then. Ms. Klinzing moved on to another state. Her job was completed. She was here to get the ratings up and she did that by sending a reporter and cameraman out to get an interview, when they had been told not to come and were not owed anything. They went uninvited to demand an interview, with the camera so close to Bob's face he had to push it away. Melissa needed a story to catch the public's eye. Melissa needed to get the Nielsen ratings up. Bob Tayar was a victim of Sweeps Month.

Bob called on our long time friend, Frank Keating, who was now Governor of Oklahoma. Back in 1978, when we opened Molly's in Tulsa and were selling liquor by the drink, illegally, Keating was the attorney who kept the restaurant open and operating. He argued that unless every other restaurant and bar was raided for illegally selling liquor, then the Alcohol Beverage Control Board couldn't continue to raid Molly Murphy's. That was harassment. For heaven's sake, the ABC Board had closed us down on our opening night in Tulsa! After over a million dollars were invested there, we needed to stay open.

Gov. Keating suggested Bob talk with his former law partner, Gary Richardson in Tulsa. Mr. Richardson had won the biggest lawsuit against the media in US history at that time, in Texas.

Gary Richardson was a personable man and agreed to take our case but needed a $10,000 retainer to cover his out of pocket expenses, then his fee would be 50% of the proceeds, if we won the case. That was great if we only had $10,000. Of all the cars we had owned, of all the property we had owned, the beautiful house we had owned, we couldn't come up with $10,000.

I knew my jewelry was a good investment, so that diamond Bob had given me appraised for much more than the $10,000. I offered it as collateral. Mr. Richardson didn't want my diamond but agreed to hold it until we could come up with the cash.

In December 1995, when we filed our suit against Palmer Communications, we held a news conference to announce this event, with our attorney standing at our side. We fully expected business to come back when the public saw that perhaps we were not the Bad Guys...we were going after the Bad Guys. What actually happened was KFOR edited the newscast to make it sound even worse than it was originally, and they ran this for the next two or three days, every newscast.

This was the nail in the coffin. Our last hope was New Year's Eve. Our business had dropped by 50%, but if we could get through until spring, when our season began, maybe things would be OK. January and February are hard months for this kind of business with the only reprieve being Valentine's Day. Normally a

New Year's Eve would mean $10,000 to $12,000 in sales. This year, in 1995, it was $3,500.

It was I who said we had to close. The staff could all be paid out of this last night's receipts. It was important to us that the staff be paid in full for their work and loyalty. January 1, 1996, the usual Staff New Year's Party was replaced by the announcement that we would no longer be open for business. Some cried, some were angry, some carried fixtures out the back door. It felt like losing a member of the family to Bob and me. Molly Murphy's was our life, our identity. We were losing this "classy, brassy, lady, Molly Murphy" as the commercials referred to our restaurant. For the next several days we tried to clean things out so there could be an auction for the equipment. The cases of steaks we expected to sell on New Year's Eve were offered back to the meat company but they wouldn't take them so we put them in our freezer at home . While we were so poor, we ate steak every night.

Part V

Surviving

A week later I was loading my car to go to Dallas for training for my new job. During this chaos I had interviewed with a Motel 6 to train as a manager. My thinking was, it would be a free place to live and pay a salary. Maybe I wasn't thinking as clearly as I should have been but we had been stripped of everything and held up for public humiliation and I wanted to get out of this town.

The night before I left, Bob, our son, daughter in law, and I all went out to dinner. Our son wanted to know exactly what I was planning. I could only say I was trying to get trained for a new job that paid $30,000 a year. No, I wasn't planning on a divorce.

I drove my 1990 Cadillac that was now 5 years old to Dallas. (I normally didn't keep a car this long, but it was a pretty car in very good condition and I couldn't afford a new one.) Bob's BMW was leased so he had turned it back the month before and found a black 1990 Cadillac, same model as mine, to drive. After all the expensive cars he had owned, he was now driving a used car...and had to have a brother get the loan for it.

There were about 20 people in the training class in Dallas for Motel 6 Management. They appeared to be mostly losers. Not one of these trainees would have been considered for even an Assistant Manager at Molly's. I began to understand why there were no really sharp trainees when I learned about the hours a manager is on duty and the responsibility they have to only be compensated $30,000 a year. No one would want this position if they could do anything else. However, I didn't think I could do anything else so when I was fired from training within two weeks, I was devastated. There was a bottle of champagne reserved for the only other woman in training and myself to drink to celebrate passing our final test, but we popped the cork that evening and I sobbed all night long.   Thank God I had left home without burning any bridges so I knew I had a place to go. The reason I was fired is still not clear to me, but it may have had something to do with my wearing my mink coat and Rolex watch to class. Well, it was January and it was cold and that was my warmest coat and the Rolex was my only watch so when the instructor told me, while appraising my jewelry and clothing, she didn't think I would enjoy living and working in a Motel 6, I agreed, of course I wouldn't enjoy it. I was just trying to survive. She told me I had until the next morning to vacate my room. That was the first time in my life I had ever been fired from a job, and it was a Motel 6! How low can you go?

Bob had decided to visit his sister who lived in California while I was in Dallas for that school. Bette lived in the Palm Springs area on a golf course. Golf had replaced Bob's racing passion. While we were living at The Greens, he took up the game at the age of 60. I was told recently by a member of The Greens who used to play with Bob that not too many golfers there wanted to play with him. I don't know if it was his ability to play the game or his temper. He would usually play alone even on the coldest days of the winter trying to perfect his game.

The house was empty when I arrived back in Oklahoma City. I was so depressed that I stayed holed up for a week only talking on the phone with my mother and my sister. Our son had moved to Indiana for a job there, and I didn't want him to worry about his mom and dad so I always tried to play down the problems we were having.

He had enough of his own. The embarrassment by The Incident didn't stop with Bob or me; my mother, my son, all of our family members were embarrassed. Our son couldn't find a restaurant management position locally so he had to relocate out of state. These times were a true test of his character and his wife's loyalty and their commitment to their marriage.

After a week or so Bob returned to Oklahoma to convince me to go back with him to California. We were using his credit card to pay for all this travel because we had no income and very little cash saved. We soon maxed the credit card out. There was no income to pay the balance so the credit card company had to write it off as a bad debt. While staying with this sister-in-law I checked my messages at home and discovered a sales position I had applied for at a downtown hotel had left a message for me to interview with them. It was exciting enough for us to rush back to Oklahoma City so I could go for this interview. What a disappointment when all the hotel manager wanted to do was talk about The Incident and hear my story. I don't believe he ever really considered me for the job.

We went through our storage unit and sold anything of value that we no longer needed to raise a few thousand dollars to pay our basic living expenses. I had to work and nothing seemed to open up for me so I began doing temporary jobs. I had never learned how to use the computer. Oh, I took the course when I was getting my Associate Degree but I sucked up to the instructor just in time to come out with a "B" but never actually learned how to use the computer. Finally I was hired by a health insurance company for customer service. I was there three months when I quit during an emotional outburst because the callers were so rude to me. No one ever calls their insurance company to say, "Have a nice day". They call because they are angry the insurance didn't pay their claim, as they should be, because I know from that experience that insurance companies will let a claim go as long as possible. I didn't use my real name while employed in this customer service position. I said I was Ms. Taylor. Tayar was too easily associated with The Incident.

After quitting this job, going home, and taking a nap I felt revived and called Bob Moore Cadillac. I told the manager I had never sold anything in my life, but I had driven a Cadillac for 20 years and liked the car enough that I thought I could sell them. Since it was commission only, they had nothing to lose so they gave me a chance. It was a job that I enjoyed, and I sold several cars until the weather changed. A cold winter is not the best time to be selling cars, I learned. The first payday that I had .00 on my paycheck was when I figured I should find a salaried job. That Christmas I worked at Foley's. Ever since that experience I have tried to be extra nice to salespeople because I know their feet and back are killin' 'em.

It was while I was still selling cars that Bob left Oklahoma for good. I had gone to the dealership when he phoned about mid-morning and said he was leaving for California to stay with his sister. He wanted to know where to turn off I-40 to get to Palm Springs. I had always been the navigator on motor trips so he actually had no idea. He just always followed my directions. It wasn't a big surprise that he was leaving, because he had become very depressed being at home alone all day. When I would walk in the door in the evening, the blinds would be drawn and he would be staring at the TV. He was lethargic. If he could have been playing golf, that might have helped but there was no money for that. When his part time summer job as a golf marshall at Silverhorn Golf Course had ended, so did the free rounds. Nothing was happening on our lawsuit against KFOR. In fact, there was a court date set and Richardson Law Firm wasn't ready to try the case. They dropped it and told us they would re-file it at a later date because they were simply not prepared to go to trial so soon.

New Year's Eve, 1996, found me home alone with a bottle of champagne and in bed at 9:30 p.m. Bob had dinner at McDonald's in Palm Springs alone then returned to his sister's condo and watched TV, while his sister attended the Country Club's New Year's Eve Party. Bob didn't feel in a festive mood to join in with them. This holiday had always been a special time for us in the restaurant business and now it was just a reminder of everything lost.

This was about the time my left hip became extremely painful due to a birth defect causing me to develop a severe limp. I knew I needed to have the hip replaced, but there was no health insurance to pay for this expensive procedure. After that Christmas season at the mall, I was hired by Mathis Brothers to sell furniture. My hip and back still hurt but when showing a sofa, I would sit down on it to show how comfortable it was. I became very clever at finding a place to sit while also showing furniture.

My mother was in the hospital due to a brain hemorrhage. It became my responsibility to find a senior community for her to live after being released. In January 1997, my sister and I moved

Mama to Tealridge Senior Living Community. After getting her settled in her new apartment home, I walked out to get in my car and slipped on the black ice Oklahoma gets in January. Of course, I broke my wrist. Having no health insurance I just ignored it for three days before phoning my physician and asking for a painkiller. He wouldn't let me have any without getting an X-ray, so next came a cast. Between my hip that needed to be replaced, the scoliosis in my back, and my broken right wrist I felt lousy. One morning after dropping by my mother's house to see if the "For Sale" sign was still there, I was sitting at the stop sign on Villa and had a decision to make; go to Mathis Brothers and try to get through another day or go home and go to bed. I decided to go home and go to bed. I phoned in sick.

The next day I had my car parked at the cleaners while I went inside to fetch something I had dropped off and returned to my car to find a woman from the bank inside trying to lock the doors saying the car was repossessed. Knowing the back door lock wouldn't lock, I opened it, planted myself in the backseat and refused to move, until the police officer with her told me he would put a cast on my other wrist if I didn't get out immediately...and this is with my cane in the seat beside me! What a compassionate guy. The bank had not gone through the proper legal actions to repossess my car, which had been put up as collateral for that payroll we had to cover. I knew they were in the wrong to do this to me. An attorney we had used for other things verified this but advised me to let it go...in order to prove they did this illegally I would need to hire an attorney and knowing I had no money, that would be a bad idea. So I walked home carrying my cleaning, feeling sorry for myself. When no white knight came to my rescue, I came up with a plan.

I told Bob I would join him in California. My sister loaned me $4000 to buy my car from the bank, I rented space in a storage unit for our personal belongings, arranged for a company to have an estate sale after I vacated my sister-in-law's house and then waited until the cast could be removed from my wrist so I could make the 1,200 mile drive to Palm Springs. California, here I come!

Coming down is hard, but once you're down, it's OK...the only way is up from there. Before I left Oklahoma City, Bob phoned and asked me to be sure to bring the canister holding Sapphire's ashes with me. Sapphire was his black Lab that he loved so much that when she died, he had her cremated and kept her ashes in his office with her purple collar draped around the canister. I took it with me.

I had $500 in my wallet, but I had several credit cards in my name that had been mailed to me through the years which had never been used. I thought they might come in handy some day, and they sure did, especially now that Bob no longer had any credit left on his. When I stopped by to tell Mama good-bye and hugged her, I knew this was one of those moments where my life was making a major turn. Tears came to my eyes as I left her apartment. I had always been the one to take her to lunch and shopping because my sisters worked and I was more available to her. Daddy had died several years earlier.   I felt I was abandoning Mama...but you do what ya' gotta do.

There were many things to consider as I headed west on I-40. Bob was working at PGA West Golf Course as a golf marshall and loved being able to play golf there. In fact, he had played one day with O.J. Simpson, just after he was found not guilty for murdering his wife and her friend. We had watched that trial every day and felt O.J. was guilty but a celebrity is a celebrity, so Bob had his picture taken with him before the day was over and got O.J.'s autograph on the score card. Bob said O.J.'s hands were huge and he did indeed have a great deal of charisma. He could understand why he was so popular.

Bob and O.J. Simpson at PGA West, La Quinta, CA 1996

Bob was staying with his sister in her spare bedroom until one of her condominiums became vacant for us to live in, rent free. We agreed on a fast food restaurant near her house on I-10 for him to meet me, and I would follow him to the country club where she lived. I remember sitting in a booth, enjoying the beautiful flora the desert offers in the springtime and seeing a shiny, black Cadillac pull up outside and a slender, very tan man with beautiful white hair that sparkled in the sunlight get out. I thought, Wow! That's a good lookin' guy! It was my husband.

He was not the same person who had left Oklahoma three months earlier. That depressed individual was now radiant and excited about our spending time in this golf haven until our case went to trial and we won the millions he knew we would win from Palmer Communications. Bob was always a great date. He enjoyed being in the best places, so we went to lunch in Rancho Mirage at a fabulous resort and shared a cold salmon salad that couldn't be matched in Oklahoma City. Then we went to his sister's condo and unloaded my car.

It took me 10 days to find a job. OK. It wasn't the best job but it paid $6.50 an hour as an assistant in a weight loss studio. I would help those chubby, well-to-do ladies with the equipment and after closing, I ran the vacuum. (I remembered having two cleaning ladies twice a week not too many years earlier, and they were better paid than I...they earned $10 an hour.) However, the owner eventually read my resume and seeing that I had worked in sales in a car agency, she moved me into a sales position. Soon I was Sales Manager. My salary and commissions equaled about $24,000 a year. My first two-week paycheck was less than I used to pay for a David Hayes suit at the Jean-Lee Dress Shop.

Bob had worked at PGA West Golf Resort just over 90 days, making him eligible for health insurance. He had Medicare by this time but I had nothing, so I was able to use their Cobra to have my first hip replacement the next summer at Eisenhower Hospital in Palm Desert. Thank God for that. I had been limping around long enough. The weight loss sales ended when the business closed and one of my clients offered me a job in her vacation rental business. I learned a little about a computer and worked at this job for two years. During this time Bob had 15 jobs. Mostly they were no brainers. He liked being a golf marshall so he could play free golf, but some jobs were in restaurants as the maitre d'. For a brief time he was floor manager at the Fabulous Palm Springs Follies, a Palm Springs attraction where all the cast members are over 50 years old. He loved working among the celebrities and the show biz atmosphere, wearing his tux every night. He did cut a handsome figure. The producer of the Palm Springs Follies, Rif Markowitz, had an ego about the size of Bob's and it wasn't long before they clashed. Bob was out of a job again. Normally he would be released because he would try to run the place he was employed by. Truth be known, he probably did know better how things should be run, but that wasn't his job so he would be fired. He encouraged me to get a job at the country club where his sister had bought us a condo, using her credit for the mortgage and us making the payments, so that he could again play golf without the hefty greens fee. I was able to get hired at Cathedral Canyon Country Club as a receptionist/administrative assistant. Poor Bob. He began trying to run the golf course, the restaurant, the snack bar, and the cocktail lounge. Since my manager was being paid to run those departments, he told me that Bob could no longer play golf there. He was banned from the Country Club.

This naturally caused Bob to become very angry and again depressed. Our lawsuit had been dragging for three or four years now. He fussed with our attorneys because they didn't keep us informed and they didn't seem to be pushing for a trial date. He fussed with servers in restaurants. He had road rage. He passed one car and gave the driver the obscene gesture, then saw the driver was wearing the collar...he was a priest.

There were other times when Bob would decide we should go out on the town and try to forget about all the problems we were having while trying to survive until the trial. He was becoming more and more certain we would be awarded millions. His Social Security and my paycheck didn't actually cover nights on the town or dinner at Mortons, so my credit cards were used. Well, they were used for many other things too, like flying to see our new grand baby in Ohio and some furniture for the condo. Before long, making only minimum payments, we were $20,000 in debt.

Three thousand dollars of that was for our son to take a course in computers. He learned, after working in about four different chain restaurants, that it is no fun if your Dad doesn't own the business. He discovered he had an interest in computers so, after spending at least $50,000 for his private school, and no telling how much at OU for his degree in Journalism, it was this $3,000 course that gave him his present career at J.P. Morgan/Chase as a Senior Network Engineer. He has done very well.

Maybe if I were a better person I could have avoided our divorce, but it got to a point where I just couldn't continue to go home and not know if I would find an angry husband, a depressed husband, or a husband who wanted to go out to celebrate. It was all very stressful. The debt we were accumulating was worrying me. I truly tried to manage that debt, but Bob carried one of those credit cards and golf is expensive, even if you are using the discount coupons clipped from the newspaper.

One day after an awful argument, I asked around at the Country Club for a place for me to rent, alone. Seems a lady had an extra bedroom she would let for $500 a month right there on the golf course, so I rented it and moved out on April 12, 2000. My son's 34th birthday. Being told his parents are separating was not a very nice gift for him, and I'm sorry about that. I didn't really intend to get a divorce. We had been married 37 years. Since he had nothing else to do and he was very angry that I left him, Bob began following me. It seemed the only thing I could do to get out of the mess we were in at this time was file for divorce. I needed to feel I had some control over my life and some peace.

After filing the papers, I drove by the condo and saw him sitting inside. It was Father's Day. I stopped and went in to visit a little while. I hated to see him there alone and I knew I could come back if I wanted, but being there was too depressing and pulling me down, too. So I gave him a long hug, knowing it would be the last as husband and wife, and left.

A few weeks later he was found on the street, passed out, while jogging. He had a heart attack. A stint was imbedded and he was released from the hospital. I knew nothing about this until several weeks later. He warned our son and his sister not to tell me of this incident. They didn't. Of course, if I had known, I would have been there for him and probably not gone on with the divorce. I would have felt a responsibility to nurse him back to health. It was best I didn't learn of this until after he was well.

Neither of us could afford an attorney so we just represented ourselves in divorce court. The only asset was the lawsuit and it had been thrown out of court. We were waiting for our attorneys to appeal it. As far as my jewelry, he had about the same amount and the furniture, well, what little we had there in California wasn't worth much and he needed it. So, the only thing I asked the court for was half interest in the lawsuit, which was worthless at that time. I was awarded that...as well as all the debt on the credit cards because they were in my name. Oh, sure, Bob was ordered to pay half, but he had no money other than his Social Security check. When he finally did begin selling golf carts, he worked on commission only and there was no way I could make him pay $12,000 to me for the debt. About six months later, I filed bankruptcy.

When I say I filed bankruptcy, I mean I, with no legal help, filed bankruptcy. If I'd had the money to pay an attorney, I wouldn't have been filing bankruptcy! Having worked with legal counsel for Molly's Chapter 11, I felt confident that I could do this myself since there really wasn't much to list other than the credit card debt and some debt to the Tayar Family that I felt was Bob's responsibility.

One day at the Country Club where I was working a nice man playing golf   struck up a conversation with me. After getting to know each other he said he was willing to share his lovely home for a very reasonable amount of rent, $300 a month. He drove me to

Riverside, California, where I sat at the cubicle with tears streaming down my face as I did the necessary paperwork to end this debt. He also helped me get a used Toyota that was in driving condition. My poor old 1990 Cadillac was now 10 years old and every time I turned around, it needed some work done on it. My friend had to get the loan on the car, and I paid him. I was able to pay him off much earlier than expected because I soon became Membership Director at the Club and then began a totally new career in Senior Living Sales. I was doing only slightly better than the $6.50 an hour I started out earning. I still bought my clothes on the sale rack at T.J. Maxx, and had to manage my money very carefully.

Bob took me to dinner one evening in order to tell me all about his new idea for a restaurant, "Lillie's of San Francisco," a steak house. He always was thinking he would get another winner. I listened to him go on and on about this new venture, thinking of all the other ventures we had tried, and with no money, this would never become a reality. I finally just looked at him and said, "Bob, get on with your life. I am getting on with mine." Bless his heart. He really wanted us to get back together, but I felt we were better apart than together.

And he soon proved me right. It wasn't too much longer that he stopped by to see me at work. He was sporting Italian made trousers, and driving a new, silver Mercedes convertible...the $80,000 category, telling me he and a lady were planning a trip to Europe in a few weeks. This didn't make me feel very good since I was getting up at 4:30 a.m. to get all my physical therapy finished for my hip and be at work on time. So, where is this newfound wealth coming from? Her name was Carole. With an "E."

On one of his golf days, using the discount coupon at an upscale golf course, he was teamed up with this recently widowed, retired attorney from Chicago, and her two Jewish cousins. Of course, Bob had improved his game by now and he was great looking...and what a story he had. His delusion of a multi-million dollar lawsuit pending, and his wife, of 37 years, walked out on him when he was down...this wife that he had given everything to when he was able...walked out on poor Bob. Well, he did what he had to do. He loved the good life and now here was a woman who was begging him to enjoy it with her. Seems she wasn't too upset about being widowed and inheriting a ton of money. She just wanted an escort to spend it with.

The desert is hard on old women, especially poor old women. There are multitudes of men there looking for a woman with money of any age but if you're over 40 and not rich, forget finding too many dinner dates.

I admit, I was jealous of his good luck. He moved in with Carole and they built a $1.5 million dollar house on Rancho La Quinta Golf Course, with an infinity pool in the back, next to the guest house. They had golfing trips to Scotland and Hawaii, and gambling trips to Vegas, staying at The Bellagio. I know all this because he would send me emails at my work computer to tell me about their fabulous lifestyle. Perhaps I deserved this since I did walk out on him, but had I not left, he wouldn't have been living this high life. He should have thanked me, or maybe sent me a dozen roses.

My routine was rising at 4:30 a.m. to do my two mile walk and 30 minutes of physical therapy then getting dressed to be at work at 7:30 a.m. Not very glamorous.

During these months our lawsuit had been thrown out of court, and we were waiting on our attorneys to appeal. I desperately wanted information on the status of this action. Bob wouldn't share any news with me. That was his way of getting even with me for leaving him. There was no money to fight about, no child custody to argue. Nothing to make my life more unpleasant. So withholding information regarding the lawsuit, which was of paramount importance to me, was his only way of punishing me for leaving. But they say the best revenge is living well, so he certainly got his revenge. It didn't seem fair.

Part VI

The Trial

The first time we filed our suit against Palmer Communications was December of 1995. The court date was set sooner than Richardson Law Firm was ready to go to trial, so it was dropped to re-file later. It wasn't until April 1997, that it was again filed and Palmer Communications was summoned to Oklahoma District Court. This was just after I joined Bob in California.

Judge Blevins was assigned to the case, and he dismissed it, apparently deciding we had no valid case. Our appeal was filed in 1998, a year later, and Judge Gurich was then handling the case, when in 1999 our appeal was "affirmed in part, reversed in part, and remanded."

By the end of 1999, the case fell into the hands of Judge Karl Gray. During this 3 year period Palmer Communications asked for a summary judgment every chance they got. I'm not sure, but I believe that means they didn't want a jury trial. It didn't seem to me there would ever be a trial! After our divorce, Bob wouldn't share information with me regarding the status of the case so I would have to get my information by phoning the judge's office. This was legally Bob's case, I only held an interest in it. No one was under any obligation to tell me anything. Since my financial future depended upon the outcome, it was extremely important to me to know what was happening. Anything I was told was in legalese, and I had no idea what it meant. Apparently Judge Gray's staff tired of my phone calls, and he took a real disliking to me and to Bob. I was told that Judge Gray actually refused to hear the case after it was sent back to him after our appeal. It was then given to Judge Dixon, thank God, because he seemed to be a very fair man and heard the case.

None of us involved in the trial knew that it almost didn't happen until we were in the court house on Monday, December 10, 2001. I had been subpoenaed as a witness so I arranged to leave work to come back to Oklahoma for the trial. Bob and his live-in, Carole, went earlier to Oklahoma and spent time in Tulsa with Gary Richardson and played golf at Southern Hills Country Club. Then they checked in at the Waterford Hotel in Oklahoma City for the trial. I stayed with my sister.

Carole, being a retired attorney, wanted to sit at the legal counsel's table in an advisory role to our attorneys and be by Bob's side. Gary Richardson turned our case over to his son, Chuck, since Gary was running for governor at the time. Chuck didn't think it would be good for Bob's girlfriend to be present, at the table, in the court room, or even in the court house. She was told to wait in the car outside and not to be seen with him. I was glad of that because I didn't want to see her, but I did the first day when she was waiting outside to pick him up. My heart felt pierced. I don't know why. It just hurt.

Carole was tall, thin, had short, dark hair and looked like Bob. They could have been blood relatives they resembled each other so much. She'd even had her nose snipped, as Bob had done.

The basis for all this legal action was that on November 18, 1995, two women took a friend to Molly Murphy's and were disappointed. It does sound silly.

That first lawsuit filed in 1995 was really three suits: one for Bob, one for me, and one for Molly Murphy's. Mine was thrown out because I wasn't even there so I was not hurt. Wish someone had explained to me that I wasn't hurt, because it sure did feel like I was.

Molly's suit was eliminated because it was in Chapter 11, and there was no need to pursue further. We felt differently because we had just come up with, on the exact day of The Incident, November 18, 1995, our plan for recovery by Spring 1996. According to the court transcript, we could not discuss Molly's lost profits over lost business because Mollly's was not a party to the suit. (This would hurt us on determining the amount of damages later.)

Bob Tayar's suit was the only one remaining. It, too, had changed dramatically. Originally there were several charges against Channel 4. There was Defamation, False Light, Intrusion on Seclusion of Privacy, Intentional Emotional Distress, Tortuous Interference with Business, and Malicious Prosecution.

Every newscast run by Channel 4, during this time of reporting The Incident after our filing suit, the TV station would run a list of every lawsuit that had ever been filed against them and show they had been dismissed. Normally that means it was settled out of court, but to the average TV viewer, it is interpreted as being dropped for other reasons … like no case.

Our suit came down to basically one charge, Defamation. That was due to broadcasting using these phrases:

1. "You could call it the case of Double Coupon Double Cross."
2. "The victims are Cindy Trent and Debbie Pester."
3. "...The waiter turned the tables on them."
4. "...slugging photographer Brad Riggin..."
5. "Tayar went on the offensive."
6. Videotape of Plaintiff's (Bob's) arrest, which implies that he is a criminal.
7. "It ended with an all out attack..."
8. "...even though it was Molly Murphy's who created the problem."
9. "Why are a Channel 4 reporter and photographer on an Oklahoma City restaurant owner's Hit List? We'll tell you."

The broadcast, when taken as a whole, portrayed Bob Tayar as dishonest, unscrupulous, and a double-crossing businessman and person.

On the other hand, Channel 4 was contending that Bob Tayar suffered no injury to his reputation. The news reports were not false or defamatory. Nor were they negligent in preparing and presenting the news reports.

These were the two sides' arguments as we began trial on Monday, December 10, 2001, six years after The Incident.

I arrived at the courthouse that cold, windy morning wearing my best suit - one I had bought on sale with my employee discount when I worked at Foley's that Christmas a few years earlier. I sat on a bench in the hall outside the courtroom. Bob arrived and sat next to me looking a little shabby, very unlike him. Where was the Italian suit? Where was his Rolex President gold watch? Apparently, he had been told by our attorneys not to flaunt his newfound wealth. That wasn't a problem for me.

He did look very different than when he had stopped by to see me one day at the Country Club a few months earlier wearing three rings, his Rolex, a gold link bracelet, and a gold chain around his neck. He asked if I thought he was wearing too many rings. I said, "Bob, you look like Sammy Davis, Jr. when he appeared on The Tonight Show." He removed one ring. It was a star sapphire he had worn for years. He now was wearing a new gold, diamond and ruby ring in its place. He explained it was a gift from Carole. She had one exactly like it. The stones were from her deceased husband's jewel mine in Africa. I asked if that meant they were going steady.

Bob had a suggestion for me. He would be sitting at the table with counsel in the middle of the courtroom. As I walked past him to the witness stand, when I was called to testify, perhaps I could pat him on the back because it would look good to the jury and the court. I gave him a look that said, Absolutely NOT! He paused then said, "I guess grabbing my crotch is out of the question." We both broke out in laughter because it reminded us of a joke we had thought incredibly funny years ago.

Finally we were ready to begin the trial. Bob went inside the closed doors of the courtroom but I was to spend the next week sitting on the bench outside, except for the time I was testifying. I was eager to learn what was happening so every time they adjourned for a break I was there to have Bob give me a report. After briefing me, he would then go over to a corner and call his Retired Lawyer, Steady Girlfriend to give her a report. At least I didn't have to be intimidated by her being there in person. I'm always intimidated by tall, thin women.

Toward the end of the first day I was called to the witness stand. I didn't grab Bob's crotch on my way to the chair. However, when our attorney, Keith Ward, who was on the Richardson team, began to ask me about our marriage and the divorce, I began sobbing uncontrollably, though no one prompted me to do it.   I never wanted to be divorced. I wanted to be the example. The exception. The couple who celebrated their 50th wedding anniversary. But things just became too stressful.

Judge Dixon called it a day when I couldn't quit crying, and I completed my testimony on Tuesday. The jest of my contribution to the trial was my account of the change The Incident had on Bob - his depression, his humiliation, the stress on him and our marriage. After my testimony was completed I was banished back to the bench in the hallway.

Anthony Foster was next on the witness stand. Mr. Foster has died now, and I know it isn't nice to say bad things about the deceased, but I'm only telling what was in the court reporter's transcript. Anthony Foster had gone through personal bankruptcy himself only a few years earlier. He acknowledged knowing how it leaves a person feeling stripped of everything. He also admitted that he became angry on the phone with Bob Tayar because, "You don't hang up on the news media." He decided to go find out why Bob Tayar hung up on him. That was the story he was after. It had nothing to do with the two women and their free coupon. He knew he was the man with a camera, the man with the ability to put someone live on TV, the man with the power in the relationship.

Next to testify was our Expert Witness, Bob Losure. Mr. Losure was a Tulsan who had been an anchor at CNN Headline news for 11 years. This didn't impress, or perhaps it DID impress, KFOR's attorneys, because they argued that Bob Losure really didn't have the background qualification to express the kinds of opinions he would be asked if he was allowed to be our Expert Witness. We did win that argument. Mr. Losure's testimony referred to the Code of Ethics for the Society of Professional Journalists. In his opinion those standards were violated by KFOR's news department. He felt they were negligent about the facts..

One of the criteria for reporting is, "Showing compassion for those who may be affected adversely by news coverage. Use special sensitivity when dealing with children and inexperienced sources or subjects."

It also says, "Journalists should be honest, fair, and courageous in gathering, reporting, and interpreting information." And,

" journalist should make certain that headlines, teasers, do not mislead or misrepresent the fact."

The type of journalism used in the area Melissa. Klinzing came from in Florida was very aggressive. When she arrived in Oklahoma City, KWTV-Channel 9 was rated No. 1. KFOR needed "a kick in the pants." The "flash and trash" and "if it bleeds, it leads" type of news casting was implemented and it sure enough worked. The "guilty building syndrome," (stand in front of a building where nothing has happened, but it looks guilty just because the reporter is standing in front of it for the camera) worked in Oklahoma City. KFOR went from No. 3 rating to No. 1! And it sold in 1997.

The cameraman, Brad Riggin, was called next, but his testimony didn't amount to much.

The third day he reported to the court I was talking with a juror. I didn't know the lady who sat next to me on my bench outside the courtroom was a juror. Her coat covered her badge. Yes, she sat with the jury while I was on the witness stand, but I saw the jury as a whole, not individually. I simply didn't recognize her when she sat down and began to make small talk early that morning while she waited for the courtroom door to be opened. It was when I saw Brad Riggin walk in and give us a look that I interpreted as "GOTCHA," that I realized the situation and moved.

When Judge Dixon called me into his chambers I felt like a child being called into the principal's office. Judge Dixon asked what it was we discussed and all I could remember was the weather. But my mind was racing...Oh, my God! what if the case is thrown out of court, and we all have to go home without having our trial. I would be in big trouble with my former husband and his Retired Lawyer, Steady Girlfriend, as well as the Richardson Law Firm if I caused a problem on this case. How many more years would we have to wait to get back in court...or maybe they wouldn't even let us come back. I offered to take a lie detector test to prove that I didn't discuss the case with the juror. That wasn't necessary. Judge Dixon then spoke with the juror and she told pretty much the same story as I did so she was dismissed and the alternate was called in to replace her. Big sigh of relief from me!

The fourth, and final, day of witnesses, Bob Tayar was called to testify. In past years Bob's arrogance and temper made him a bad witness. This time it was apparent his Retired Lawyer, Steady Girlfriend had insisted his physician prescribe some sort of tranquilizer because he didn't come off as arrogant, according to my sister, who was inside the courtroom during his testimony. She said Bob sounded like an old man who was slightly confused. The crux of his testimony was that we had given out many of these COMP gift certificates through the years, and this was the first time we had a problem. Also, Molly Murphy's had been the recipient of an award of being selected one of the top 50 best restaurants in the United States in 1991, just four years prior to The Incident. He also told how our balance sheet would have been cleaned up by pring of 1996, according to our plan for Chapter 11, Reorganization. This balance sheet was what he felt had kept us from being successful in expanding Molly Murphy's out of state.

The video Brad Riggin had made was then played, and Bob was told to count the number of times he told Foster and Riggin to get off the property. It was 17 times.

Then Bob was asked how much business Molly's lost after this video was shown on KFOR's newscast. He answered 50%. The final question was whether we were able to pull out of bankruptcy after The Incident.

"No, Sir. That did us in. We closed."

That was the end of testimony. On the fifth day both attorneys gave their final arguments. The jury was given instructions.

While the jury was in its quarters deciding our fate, I sat with my sister, Darlene, and promised God that if He would allow us to win this case, I would always be sweet. Never again would I be hostile, rude, or obnoxious in my life. Fortunately, I had not yet made that promise when I encountered Bob's Retired Lawyer, Steady Girlfriend.

After the jury left the courtroom, Bob asked my sister and me to go for coffee and wait for the verdict together. We agreed. Then Bob's cell phone rang. He walked away to talk, then returned saying he couldn't join us after all and excused himself. OK. Darlene and I walked to the vending machine area downstairs and who do we see inside the courthouse but Bob sitting with his Retired Lawyer, Steady Girlfriend. She wasn't to set foot inside the courthouse!

I found our attorney. He explained that now that the jury was deliberating, Bob's RL-SGF wanted to be inside the courtroom sitting with Bob for the verdict. I had been sitting in the hallway all week on my hardwood bench and this was my turn to be inside the courtroom to hear the verdict. Did I want to share that moment with Bob's Retired Lawyer, Steady Girlfriend? This was MY life. It had nothing to do with Bob's RL-SGF. No. I didn't want her there. Well, he explained to me that it may take a court order to keep her out, and it was too late in the day to get that document. I explained to him that if she was inside the courtroom, what Bob did to Foster was nothing compared to what I would do to Bob's RL-SGF! I guess he believed me because she wasn't there. That's when I made my promise to God about always being a sweet woman the rest of my life, if He would just let us win.

The jury found in our favor. They declared damages to be $350,000. Then they were sent back to determine Punitive Damages. I didn't know this, but, in Oklahoma, Punitive Damages can't exceed actual damages, so that meant we were awarded $700,000. I was elated and confirmed to God that I would be sweet hence forth. Bob was disappointed. He and his Retired Lawyer, Steady Girlfriend has convinced each other that he would win millions.

Since I had been adamant in my demand that RL-SGF not be in the court room when the jury came back with the verdict, she went back to their hotel. I offered Bob a ride as everyone was leaving the courthouse and he accepted. When I stopped in front of The Waterford, Bob and I looked at each other in the darkness of the car and began to hug. It was a hug we had waited six years to give each other. We had won. Our lives had completely changed . We had been through emotional hell. No amount of money can compensate for all that, but we did have the satisfaction that we had won.

A few years later I located a member of the jury and asked him how the jury arrived at the sum of $350,000 for damages. He said they simply didn't have enough information to go on, so they thought that would be the amount we would have earned had we stayed open during that time. Let's see...$350,000 divided by six years...$58,000 a year...divided by two (Bob and I shared equally)...$29,000 a year. Well, we got some interest because Palmer Communications appealed the decision, and it was another two years before we won that and they paid us.

I also asked the juror what the jury discussed about our case. He said all the witnesses for KFOR came off as very self righteous, and they had made a big deal over nothing. The crime didn't fit the punishment, so to speak. I agreed.

Part VII

The Waiting

After the trial, I returned to the desert and my position as Membership Director at the Country Club. Bob and I had been able to maintain a friendly relationship in order to share information about our son and granddaughters. There were two of those now. They lived in Ohio, so I wasn't able to see them often. One of my two weeks of vacation time each year had to be spent visiting Oklahoma and my mother who was now over 90 years old and residing in a nursing home.

Bob and his RL-SGF visited Ohio frequently on their way to New York or Europe. She was fortunate to be a wealthy widow. I began telling people I always wanted to be a wealthy widow, too, but Bob struggled every time I put the pillow over his head, so I finally had to divorce him. And I didn't divorce very well.

Bob was experiencing a wonderful lifestyle; one that he and I should have been sharing. I had always thought we would travel to Europe some day but here I was still struggling from payday to payday. My friend had raised my rent and my other hip had to be replaced, causing me to lose some time on the job. I was praying the State Supreme Court would find in our favor and my share of the judgment would be a nest egg for me to help with retirement. Palmer Communications had filed an appeal after our win, so we knew it was going to be another long wait until they made a decision.

One day I got a letter in the mail from an attorney representing Bob offering me $50,000 for my share of the judgment. That was about 20% of what was due me if we won the appeal. They also wanted me to sign a document saying that I relinquished any future attempts for spousal support. You see, when I filed my own divorce papers, I left a box unchecked. It meant that I could go back at any time and ask the courts for spousal support, should Bob ever have an income. Fat chance of that. I didn't leave it unmarked because I was smart. It was simply that I overlooked it. I didn't really believe Bob would ever have an income and if he did, he was smart enough to hide it from me so I could never get a part of it. I had no intention of trying to get spousal support from him at any time in the future. And their offer of $50,000 for my share of the judgment was not something I was interested in accepting.

Apparently Bob and his RL-SGF thought I was so miserable and poor that I would jump at that offer. The fact is, I grew up without money. I wasn't lazy. I didn't mind working to support myself. I rejected their kind offer.

I can picture Bob and his RL-SGF now, sitting on their patio at twilight next to the pool, gazing out to the golf course greens, sipping their cocktails and scheming to get rid of me and my share of the lawsuit. They didn't need my share of the money. It was nothing compared to what Carole inherited from her husband when he died. I felt they simply wanted me to have nothing. As our attorney, Chuck Richardson, explained to me during the trial when Carole was throwing a hissy fit to be in the courtroom, she hated me because I had a piece of Bob's heart for 37 years. She wished I didn't exist.

They came up with a plan. One day while I was at work I was delivered a summons to court. This was unbelievable. They were suing me. After I helped win the lawsuit, I was being sued for my share of it. They listed several reasons why I shouldn't have any portion of this money.

One was that Bob would never have given me half of the suit if he'd had legal counsel during our divorce. Of course, Bob didn't GIVE me anything. The judge awarded me half of the suit, and I had no legal counsel either!

Another reason was that I was negligent when I filed my bankruptcy and didn't list the lawsuit as an asset. OK. Maybe they got me there. I had no legal counsel for that either and maybe I screwed up. There were some other charges equally as ludicrous. I was livid.

During all this divorce mess, I had tried not to pull our son into having to take sides, but this time I needed him. I read the charges in the suit against me, and he advised me to get a good attorney. In California, attorneys aren't cheap and I lived from payday to payday. My friend/landlord forwarded me $2,500 and I hired a lawyer. It took me five months to repay him.

For that $2,500 I was able to hire ten hours from Ms. Sternlieb to represent me in court. Ms Sternlieb was a tiny woman who had an incredible wardrobe. I realized my fee was going to pay for another one of those designer outfits, as I sat in my sale rack suit from T. J. Maxx. I remembered how it felt to be wearing one of those exquisite suits.

Ms. Sternlieb read the charges made against me by Bob and immediately told me I was in the right. I had done nothing wrong in my filing of my bankruptcy. She thought I'd win easily but warned me that she didn't do appeals. If I won, and Bob appealed, I'd need to find another attorney.

The day I went to court I put on my eight year old Anne Klein suit and couldn't get the skirt zipped. Guess I had put on a few pounds. Darn! The one day I would be face to face with Bob and his RL-SGF, I was fat! I had to change skirts and looked ridiculous wearing a skirt that didn't match the jacket, but I didn't have time to completely change clothes because I didn't want to be late for court.

I was already seated when my accusers (I'm sure RL-SGF was a big part of this) sauntered down to the last available bench, on the front row. Bob's catch in his shoulder must have been giving him trouble as it did when he was under stress, because he kept reaching back to rub it. I could see the bald spot with the undyed white hair around it on the back of RL-SGF's head. And I still felt intimidated. Tall, thin women always intimidate me even when they are sitting down.

After we answered the Judge's roll call, Ms. Sternlieb summoned me to the hallway. The plaintiff's attorney had offered a settlement before our case was called. Bob was offering to drop the suit if I would agree not to ever ask for spousal support.

Ms. Sternlieb wanted to argue the case being confident she could win. On the other hand, if I did win, Bob was sure to appeal and I'd have to hire another attorney to handle the appeal. Also, it would most likely be afternoon before our case would be called, and I really needed to get back to work. I also wondered just how many of those ten, prepaid legal hours had been used. I didn't want to acquire more costs.

It didn't bother me to sign off on spousal support because Bob was now a 70 year old man, and I never expected him to earn an income. If he ever did get another restaurant operating, he was smart enough to hide any income to avoid paying me any spousal support.

Bob always did have an adversity to giving me any money for my own support. Those years we were earning such a good living he had a trust set up with his sister, a brother, and our CPA as trustees who would determine how much income I would get in the event I was widowed. Our CPA told me about this and even he thought it was not fair, since I had been a major part of building our business. Bob wanted to be sure our son was the beneficiary, and that I wouldn't marry someone else and spend money he had earned. He told me that if our son wouldn't take care of his own mother, then I'd be in trouble. Whatever...

So I left the courthouse still owning my half of our won lawsuit, that was being appealed by Palmer Communications, and agreeing never to ask for spousal support from Bob. And owing $2,500 to my friend for paying my legal fees up front. For $2,500 I would have signed over spousal support without all this legal stuff. What was the point of all this? I soon found out. They were planning to marry.

I recall driving down May Avenue once and a marquee at Mayfair Shopping Center read, "A Widow and Her Money Are Soon Married."

And so she was. There is no doubt in my mind that had Carole been without funds, there would not have been a third Mrs. RLT. (There was a brief marriage before me, young love, no children.)

My daughter-in-law told me the details regarding this upcoming event. Carole had been diagnosed with Stage III lung cancer. She told Bob that she would take care of him for the rest of his life if he would marry her and take care of her for the rest of hers. She didn't have long to live. I'm sure Bob thought he would live another 15 to 20 years. They would be married the week-end after Mother's Day at a resort in Palm Desert, California, with our son serving as Best Man.

Bobby wasn't very happy about this arrangement. He told me he was glad his Dad had someone who afforded him the travel and a grand lifestyle, but he didn't want a Step Mom. He got one anyway. She paid for him and his family to fly to California for the week. Since she was paying the bills she controlled their time. They were allowed to visit me one day...Mother's Day. How generous of her. I couldn't compete with all this money. She was planning to fly her children and their families and our son and his family to Nassau for the next Christmas holiday. They were all just going to be one big happy family. I wasn't fitting into this picture.

To my female reading audience, Girls, it's all about money. When you are old, you better have some.

The wedding took place about one mile from where I lived. It was a sad evening for me, knowing the Rabbi was joining them in matrimony. It just didn't seem right for my husband to be marrying someone else. I somehow felt we were just fighting and eventually we'd make up. Since I didn't have any family or close friends in California, I concentrated on my new job, selling Senior Living. They even had their wedding picture in the local newspaper, like young brides and grooms. I think it was mostly for my benefit. Bob was still angry I divorced him, and Carole wanted to put me in my place.

Most of that summer they traveled, according to my daughter-in-law. But their next trip to Europe had to be cancelled because she was becoming so ill. They were married about 18 months when she died. I didn't see the obituary right away because I was in Eisenhower Hospital having a third hip replacement. The last one popped out...on the dance floor, at the Holiday Inn in Ardmore, OK, during my high school class reunion. But that's another story.

When I did read the obituary, I couldn't believe it. She referred to her husband of 42 years, simply as the father of her children. But she referred to Bob as "her special love" and "for one brief shining moment she had Camelot." I'm absolutely sure she wrote it as she was dying.

During those last three to four months while she was so ill, Bob was coming by my office to visit me and sometimes take me to lunch. He needed a friend. It's hard to live with a dying person. He, himself, was diagnosed with prostate cancer and was having radiation. I promised our son that I would see that his Dad was taken care of and not to worry about him. After all, I was selling Senior Living, which includes health care.

About a month after Carole's death, Bob asked me to meet him at Arnold Palmer's Restaurant in La Quinta for dinner. I was still recovering from that third hip replacement as I joined him at his table and rested my cane next to me. I asked about the funeral and was surprised when he said she was buried there in Palm Springs rather than in Chicago, where her husband, of 42 years, was buried. Why? Oh, she bought two plots, one for herself and one for him. And the headstone was already put up with both names on it...just the death date for Bob was missing. WHAT?

I was astounded. We were married 37 years. They were married 18 months, and they are being buried side by side. What about her children? Wouldn't they want their parents buried next to each other? It upset me so much that I got up and left the restaurant as fast as I could, considering I was using a cane.

Christmas of 2004, Bob was living alone again. He asked if I would go with him to Ohio and be with our son and his family for the holidays. I agreed. We flew together and spent five days being Citi (an Arabic word for Grandmother) and Pop. It was the last time we were all together.

Part VIII

Finally...It's Over

January of 2005 we were given our award from Palmer Communication. Over nine years after The Incident. The only advantage of having this dragged out for so long is that the judgment earned interest from the time it was filed until after the appeal was won, so we had slightly over $1 million to divide. Was it worth it? What do you think? Would you have gone through all this for that amount of money?

Bob deposited his share in a trust account to open another restaurant. I gave mine to an investor for my retirement. Bob and I had dinner at Cuistot's in Palm Desert to celebrate our win. He had gone with me to my company's Christmas party, and I joined him at his Country Club for the Super Bowl Party. We had lunch several times a week. We were friends again. He invited me to join him at any social event his Country Club had on their calendar, but I couldn't accept many of those invitations. I worked and didn't go out on "school nights." I told him he needed a new playmate who was retired. He did meet someone, and they had begun to go out occasionally but I always knew I was his first choice. He also told me that Carole's greatest fear was that after she died, he and I would get back together. And he added that she should have had that fear. I know he wanted us to be together, but there was just too much water under the bridge. I felt we could only be best friends, but I loved dating him. He made me proud to be at his side. He had all the social graces and we had so much history together. I enjoyed being with him. On a Friday evening, February 11, 2005 we had dinner at Sullivan's. Afterward, we stopped by Indian Wells Resort to hear our friend entertain. He asked if I wanted to dance. He was a fabulous date now. Anything I wanted to do, he was willing. We danced and were turning to leave to go back to our own cars and go home when the singer said, "Don't go...my next song is Eric Clapton." It was "Tears in Heaven", and Bob and I danced that last dance.

Ritz Carlton Hotel, Christmas 2004

The next day he had a golf date. I remember leaving him a message on the phone telling him some sort of cute thing our youngest granddaughter had done. That evening he took his new playmate to dinner, again at Sullivan's. After dropping her at home, he drove to Rancho La Quinta Country Club and was just inside the gated community, when he fell asleep at the wheel and drove into a palm tree.

It was about noon the next day, Sunday, that I got a call from Carole's daughter-in-law in Dallas telling me Bob was in an accident. Before I fully absorbed that information, she was telling me he died. NO! NO! NO! I was screaming "No!" as though if I screamed long enough and loud enough, she would tell me it wasn't true. My housemate took the phone and got the other details and drove me to the hospital to see him.

This couldn't be happening. He couldn't die like that. He had told me just a few days earlier that after he had been out for some drinks, he woke the next morning and saw fast food wrappers on the kitchen counter. He didn't remember going through a fast food drive-in or eating any fast food, but there was the evidence. He had been having some black outs.

When I arrived at the information desk at Palm Springs Regional Hospital and asked what room my deceased husband was in, I was told they had no record of Bob Tayar's passing. He was in room #340. What? I told her I hoped to hell she was right because someone had just called me and said he had died. Well, so much for communication in hospitals. When they finally escorted me to the room, I hardly recognized him from all the swelling. Only his beautiful white hair was as it should have been.

It's hard to get information when you are no longer Next of Kin. Our son held that position now. I was able to find out about the accident from the Sheriff Department by saying I was his wife. Well, I WAS his wife, at one time. They told me when they were called by security at the Country Club, Bob was sitting on the ground next to his wrecked Lexus. He was bleeding from having a bad cut on his lip but said he was fine and just wanted to go on home. He had just fallen asleep at the wheel. Due to his age of 72, they called for an ambulance. The Sheriff who escorted him to the hospital said Bob argued all the way. He just wanted to go home. They asked if he had been drinking and he barked, "So what if I have been?" He lost consciousness on his way for an MRI and never regained it.

He had my card in his wallet with my office and home phone numbers on it, but no one ever looked inside to find it. I hate that he died alone.

Our son had acquired a fear of flying, so he had to drive from Ohio to California with his wife, leaving the little girls in

Oklahoma with family. When he arrived, I had made all the arrangement for a memorial service at the Country Club where Bob had played golf. He had become quite a good golfer. He played in The Bob Hope Classic twice which was very thrilling for him.

The hospital had an envelope to give to Next of Kin, our son. I was with him when he opened it. There was $3,500 in one hundred dollar bills. Bob always carried a wad of cash with him as a carryover from his days of being so broke. Bobby took that to help with his travel expenses. He took the Rolex watch that his Dad always reminded him would be his some day. He took the gold coin ring I had given Bob for an anniversary gift years before and put it on his right hand. Then he took the diamond and ruby ring, and said, "I have a ring on each hand...what will I do with this?"

I said, "Honey, I'll take that. Jewelry is jewelry." I put it on my finger and felt the circle was completed.

Bob always told me that when he died he wanted family and friends to gather, have a few drinks, something to eat, and talk about how smart he was and how handsome he was. So that is what we did. I had the last picture taken of him blown up for all to see what a handsome man he had become. And we talked about his successes. He had also told me that he wanted "Wind Beneath My Wings" to be played so we did. And for me, I asked the singer to sing Frank Sinatra's "My Way," because Bob sure enough did it His Way.

After all the family went to the funeral home and viewed the body, I slipped in just before closing and said good-bye. He wasn't buried until the next week and no one was there as he was laid to rest beside his third wife. His family had all gone home, and Bobby and I had gone to Oklahoma City for a family wedding.

Our son was very philosophical about everything. He reminded me that Dad never wanted to get old or be sick. So perhaps it was better that he died as he did, after a day of golf and dinner at a nice restaurant. And perhaps it was good that he was buried there in the Palm Springs Cemetery, alongside Frank Sinatra and Sonny Bono. He always liked rubbing elbows among the rich and famous. Now he is buried next to them.

After Bob's death, it hit me that I was in the desert in California alone. Why? As long as Bob was there, married or not, there was a connection for me. Now there was none. Soon I was able to transfer to Tulsa with my company and sell Senior Living there. Well, Tulsa isn't home.

Before long I was able to move to Oklahoma City and still work in my field. And guess what? My son did take care of his mother. He bought me a house...with money his Dad got from the Palmer Communications suit.

Carole did love Bob. She was very good to him and his grand daughters. She set up a college trust fund for those little girls, and they will have plenty of money by the time they are college bound.

So, now you know "Whatever Happened to Molly Murphy?" as well as what happened to Bob and me, because we WERE Molly Murphy.